I0840851

Visions

Things and Ideas
Found in the Wild

by
The Lonesome Hillbilly

Books by the same author

The Book on Motorcycle Camping
How to Live on the Road Full Time

Places: I'm Going to Go Back There, Some Day

Roads: All Roads Lead to Roam

Friends: Two-Legs, Four-Legs, Six-Legs, Wings and Roots

Visions: Things and Ideas Found in the Wild

Elements: Elemental, Elementary

Things in Heaven and Earth
Essays from Places, Roads, Friends, Visions and Elements
with full-color illustrations

Dedicated to
Lafayette Ronald Hubbard
Who taught me how to see

Contents

Introduction

Visions - - - - - - - - - - - 1
Why - - - - - - - - - - - - 3
Knowledge - - - - - - - - - - 5

Man

Adventures - - - - - - - - - - 10
Aloneness - - - - - - - - - - 14
Doing Nothing - - - - - - - - - 16
Perception - - - - - - - - - - 18
Summer Sleep - - - - - - - - - 22
Comfortable Temperatures - - - - - - 24
Communication - - - - - - - - - 25
Cages - - - - - - - - - - - 28
Cities Are Your Friends - - - - - - 31
Having Fun - - - - - - - - - - 33
O'Havre - - - - - - - - - - - 35
A Dirty Job - - - - - - - - - - 41
Wampum - - - - - - - - - - - 43
The Micron Mind - - - - - - - - 46
Zippers - - - - - - - - - - - 49
Independence - - - - - - - - - 54

Nature

Beauty	53
Size	59
White Sound	68
Infant Mortality	72
It Just Happened	76
Life and Death	78
Transition	85
The Stump	88
Great Quest, the	93

Man and Nature

Man and Nature	96
Keeping Things Separate	99
Accomodation and Preservation	102
Mismanagement	106
It is All Up To You	109
The Duffer	113

Spirit

Meta Physics	117
Love	120
Plans and Dreams	122
Where Did the Time Go?	130
Physical and Spiritual	133
Self: Ish and Less	138
Imagine That!	141
Preferences	144
Magic in Nebraska	147

The Fairies' Siege
by Rudyard Kipling

I have been given my charge to keep –
Well have I kept the same!
Playing with strife for the most of my life,
But this is a different game.
I'll not fight against swords unseen,
Or spears that I cannot view –
Hand him the keys of the place on your knees –
'Tis the Dreamer whose dreams come true!

Ask him his terms and accept them at once.
Quick, ere we anger him, go!
Never before have I flinched from the guns,
But this is a different show.
I'll not fight with the Herald of God
(I know what his Master can do!)
Open the gate, he must enter in state,
'Tis the Dreamer whose dreams come true!

I'd not give way for an Emperor,
I'd hold my road for a King –
To the Triple Crown I would not bow down –
But this is a different thing.
I'll not fight with the Powers of Air,
Sentry, pass him through!
Drawbridge let fall, 'tis the Lord of us all,
The Dreamer whose dreams come true!

Introduction:
Visions

Many religions include practices intended to produce "visions". A true vision is not a hallucination, perceiving something that is not there, but rather an increased awareness, perceiving what is always there, but of which you have not been aware, or which you have not understood, or have misunderstood. It is observing what is *there, all* of it, then combining it, melding it, summarizing it, to produce an understanding, an insight, which you did not have before. A true vision is actually an enhanced perception which has been made possible by achieving a higher state or level of awareness.

Some people attempt to receive visions by using drugs, alcohol or other poisons. Most of these dull your awareness, often making you think you are more aware, but inducing only hallucination. Others use stress, such as fasting or exertion to exhaustion, or creating dangerous situations. These, and some of the poisons, are often successful, because they are threats to survival, and increase awareness because increased awareness raises your chances of living through the danger.

The best path to a vision is to simply raise your level of awareness, without toxins or hazards or stress. There are many things that can hold your awareness to a lower level: Ideas, beliefs, assumptions, routine and familiarity, habits of thought, mental laziness, accepting what you are told instead of evaluating data for yourself, and simply not looking. Many religions have techniques to help you spot these barriers. Find or figure out one that works for you, and *use* it. As you begin to recognize these barriers, these things that block you from understanding, you will be able to overcome them and perceive more. It is usually a very gradual process, but over time you will find yourself looking at something and seeing it as if you had never seen it before. It is like, no, it *is*, a child's sense of wonder, where everything he sees is *new*. It is looking at a tree and, instead of seeing just a tree, just one more tree among many, one tree like all of the others, you see *that tree*. It is *not* like any other tree, it is unique, an individual. That tree never existed before, and it never will again. It is not even the exact same tree that it was yesterday.

That is a vision. A very minor one, perhaps, but definitely a higher awareness than just seeing "a tree". With practice, as your awareness grows, your normal day-to-day awareness, you will see more and more of these visions, and eventually you will be able to, at will, *look* at a thing or an idea, large or small, and truly see it, perceive it, with nothing obscuring it, such as a prior idea or conception, or what you have been told, just seeing it *as it is*, right now, and understanding it. You will be able to look at an entire scene, and see it all, as a whole, as a single unit, see the forest *and* the trees. When you achieve that state, the world becomes a beautiful thing, a new and wondrous *experience*. Everything is new and full of wonder. For me, everything I ever wanted or expected (but never got) from alcohol or drugs is fulfilled simply by being more aware.

There are far more things in the world than was ever dreamt of in your, or anyone's, philosophy.

Why?

The child's favorite question is "Why?" "Why is the sky blue?" "Why is the grass green?" Lazy or foolish parents will reply "Because that is the way it is" or "Because God made it that way", or simply "Because". I used to wonder "Why?" very often, and still do, sometimes. I have learned a great deal in my lifetime, and have found that "Why?" usually is not very significant. As the Lonesome Duck (no relation) observed, "The reason for a thing is never so important as the thing itself". Sometimes the reason for a thing is very important: Knowing why diseases occur can save your life. Sometimes the reason is useful: Knowing why wood burns enables you to build a better fire, and to put one out thoroughly. Other "why"s are of no practical use to most people: What benefit is there to knowing that refraction makes the sky blue? I cannot think of a single one. But the fact that it *is* blue is useful; that is how you perceive that there are no clouds, or that clouds are breaking up.

Fortunately, finding the answer to "why?" is always interesting and usually fun. Why fortunate? Because you never truly know if the reason is going to have any practical value at all. Why do people grow old and debilitated? When we find out for certain, maybe we will be able to do something about it, slow it down or prevent it entirely. Then again, it may prove to be something we cannot affect at all. Perhaps the only way to avoid the deterioration that comes with age is to die while still young. Not a satisfactory solution.

I look at a tree and I ponder "Why?" Why is *that* tree *here*? Why not another tree, or over there? There are all kinds of learned reasons and esoteric data. The strength and direction of the wind that carried the seed, the presence of rain at the right time, the absence of wildfire till the tree could protect itself. Many reasons, but none of them matter. If not that tree, there would have been another, or two trees. If not here, then a few feet over there. All that matters is what *is*. That tree is *here*. It *is* here. Why? Because it is.

Amusing, isn't it? The brush-off answer used to conceal ignorance or to avoid the tedium of having to think or the labor and drudgery of explaining something to a child, turns out to be, ultimately, the truth. The tree is there because it is there. This may appear foolish to you, but if you think about it, if you *observe* it, you will know it to be true.

The whole forest, all of the Wilds, is like that. These trees are there because that is where they are. The mountain is there because it did not erode. The squirrel is scolding from that limb because that is where he is. They are because that is what they are. Look at the world around you. See it for what it is. Meld with it, be part of it, not a separate external observer. Only then will you understand it, comprehend it, appreciate it, even come to treasure it. And along with asking "Why?", do not neglect to ask the more important question: "Why not?"

Knowledge

It has been said that the people of twenty, thirty thousand years ago were just as intelligent as are the people of today, and maybe smarter. They just did not know as much. We have the accumulated knowledge of the many millenia, especially of the last few since we learned to write it down. We have figured out a lot of the mysteries that the Cro-Magnan and the Neanderthal speculated on in their leisure time (of which they had plenty), sitting around their fires, bellies bulging with the flesh of their latest kill, which may have been made last week. (How long does it take to eat a whole mastadon?) They would watch the skies, and hear the thunder rumbling, and probably laughed when their bellies rumbled, too. Obviously, Someone Up There had also feasted well, and was belching and digesting just like us. Yes, they had it figured out. There was quite a bit that they knew (not *believed*, but *knew*). They knew how to shape stones and sharpen and harden spears, and track and trap and kill mammoths and bears, and mice and squirrels when there was nothing larger around. And they knew there were little spirits in the woods, and in the streams, and big ones underground and huge ones in the skies, who made volcanos and earthquakes and lightning and thunder. All this and more, they *knew*.

Mostly, especially in the big things, they had it wrong. But they still learned, and passed on what they had learned, mouth to mouth, father to son, mother to daughter. They improved their weapons and tools, refined their methods and techniques, their understanding of how to better control, or at least make tolerable, the world around them. They had their specialists to handle the more involved tasks, such as flint-knapping and dealing with spirits. We look back indulgently at their witch-doctors and medicine-men (not *real* doctors dealing with *real* medicine), at their quaint superstitions and their laughable delusions about the workings of the Universe, but we forget (if we ever realized) that their shamans were not cunning opportunists fooling the ignorant commoners with clever tricks, but honest and sober practitioners of arts already ancient, applying knowledge which they had spent decades learning, working as apprentices to their old masters, preserving lore painfully gathered by trial and error. Much of their knowledge was false, mistaken, such as the effect of the phase of the moon on healing or gathering herbs or planting crops. On the other hand, most of the application worked, or they would not keep doing it. It just did not work for the reasons they thought it did. The ancient Greeks, for example, knew (*knew*, mind you) that diseases were caused by tiny demons called *keres*. The keres got into the body and disrupted its functions, and that made the person sick. If you came into contact with a sick person, you had to wash afterward, so that the water would scare away the demons. Today we know (*know!*) that diseases are not caused by tiny demons but by microscope creatures called *bacteria* and *viruses*, and that washing simply washes these demons, I mean *germs*, away. You see, the Greeks had the application correct, but their understanding of *why* it worked was just ignorant silly superstition.

You do not need to go back hundreds or thousands of years to find superstition to be prevalent. It is with us all of the time, and probably always will be. It need not involve ghosts or demons or anything supernatural; superstition has best been defined as an effort, for lack of education, to find pertinent data in too wide a zone or to fix the attention upon irrelevant data. Put another way, if a person does not understand something, he will make up an explanation. You have done it, though you may not be aware of it. I have done it myself. In fact, as a child, I did it constantly, till I learned the error of it. When I was about ten, I wondered about the difference between an engine and a motor. I had no explanation, so I invented one. You have the gasoline engine and the electric motor. Okay, clearly an engine produces its own power, while a motor is supplied with energy from an external source. Logical. Wrong. Superstition. A bit of research provided the accurate data: *Any* machine is an engine. The word is from the Latin "*ingen(ium)*, nature, innate, quality, especially mental power, hence, a clever invention" (from the Random House College Dictionary, revised edition, 1984). A *comb* is an engine, a clever invention for aligning hair neatly. A motor is an engine for providing motion.

The partner of Superstition, or perhaps I should say *accomplice*, is Authority The less that is accurately known about a field, the more authoritarian that field will be. "Dr. So-And-So is recognized as the greatest authority in this field, and he says it is true, so I do not need to look at your data. I *know* it is wrong." When the brand new theory of Continental Drift was first introduced, it was scorned. The geologists *knew* that the continents had always been where they are, and could not possibly move; they were far too big, and there was no mechanism to cause them to move. The apparant similarities between some coastlines, the way they almost fit together like pieces of a crossword puzzle, was simply coincidental. But today, we have a whole new science called Plate Tectonics, we know where the continents lay over the past billion years or so, and we know why they moved, and that they still move, and where they will be over the next few hundred million years. We even measure their annual movement.

One hundred years ago we knew many things. You cannot travel faster then the speed of sound. You cannot reach the moon. The automobile will never replace the horse. Fifty years ago we knew many things. If you go swimming within half an hour of eating, you will get a cramp. Eating fats causes heart disease. We only have enough petroleum to last thirteen years. We are in a period of climate change, and global temperatures are dropping. You can look these things up. A little research will show you, we did not *believe* these things, we *knew* them; they were positive, proven *facts*. At least, the Authorities told us they were proven facts, and we naturally believed them.

Of course, we know better today. The amount we know now is vast, truly vast. We understand the Universe, and economics. Why, we understand almost everything! I, personally, have a vast amount of knowledge. There is one thing, though, which I do not know: How much of what I know, *know*, mind you, is wrong?

The first step on the path to Wisdom is understanding and accepting that it is always possible that, in anything, you may be wrong.

Man

Adventures

Long ago, a callow youth of twenty-two set out to have an Adventure. He was young, and he knew everything. He had been raised under the constant threat of nuclear war, and could clearly see that Civilization was soon to fall, so he had been studying Wilderness Survival for nearly a decade. He knew, from books, how to live off the land: What he could eat, what to avoid, how to build shelters, how to make fire without matches, how to find his way by stars and sun. He knew it all. From books. But he also had the very first glimmering of wisdom, for he realized that the knowing and the doing were different things, though he did not yet know how different. And thus he gathered together his gear, disposed of his other belongings, and quit his job as a cook. He set out from Cape Cod, Massachusetts with twelve hundred dollars in traveler's checks and too much gear on his back and headed west. He was fine till he reached the mountains, where he learned that a pair of blankets was not, contrary to Nessmuk and the Boy Scout Handbook, sufficient to sleep warmly in the mountains in April. They were effective to prevent chattering teeth, if you bit on them. The very next day he bought a down sleeping bag.

When he found a west-flowing waterway, he inflated his rubber kayak, loaded his gear, and began the easy travel. It was a narrow creek, six or eight feet wide and just barely deep enough, with an occasional island splitting the stream. At the first large island, he spent too long deciding which channel to follow, and was caught broadside on the island head. This flooded the boat and soaked him and all of his gear with very cold water. A writer once described adventure as something bad happening to someone else a long way away. He was right about the "bad" part. The young man proceeded to the first acceptable camping spot, unloaded and spread his gear to dry. Then he laid a fire and, because his matches were wet, got out his magnifying glass and learned another lesson: Burning glasses do not work under a full overcast. Next day he bought a Zippo lighter and some waterproof matches.

He learned quickly, for he had much to learn, from painful lessons. He stopped early enough to set up camp for the night. He avoided camping on the damp ground next to a stream. He gathered *lots* of firewood, so he would not run out and have to seek more in the dark. He broke camp early so he had plenty of time to travel before stopping early. He learned that wet is okay, and cold is okay, but wet and cold together is bad. He learned that Tonto was a twit. "White man build big fire, sit away from it. Indian build small fire, sit on top." Small fire make much smoke, no heat. The smart man builds a big fire to get a good bed of coals, *then* keeps it small. Medium-small.

And the lessons paid off, in a big way. Drifting down the a tributary of the Allegheny River, he was overtaken by a half-dozen boys in a pair of canoes. It was just about stopping time and they were passing a beautiful large green meadow about three feet above the water level. The boys wanted to stop there, but the youth shook his head. "Too low", he said, knowing it would be damp. They found a spot a half-mile farther downstream, where they had to climb a fifteen foot bank at a forty-five degree angle. That night it rained, and the river rose to within two feet of their camp. The boys were awe-struck; the grassy meadow was *very* damp.

He left the river in Pennsylvania when the waters grew too foul, and learned to hike. He learned to stop and rest for five minutes every hour, and to walk more slowly when going uphill. He learned what made a good staff, and discarded half of his gear. He learned to be wary of mice and squirrels, and to hide his food where they could not reach it. He learned to sleep on hard ground by contouring it to fit his body. He learned to keep his feet clean and dry. You can imagine the painful lessons that taught him these and many other things. Adventures. Some annoying, some deadly, such as the time he had to jump from a ledge to a handhold, over a hundred foot drop to uncomfortably sharp rocks, because his ignorance and carelessness had left him with no other way out. But the youth survived, and learned the greatest lesson of all, that there was one *hell* of a lot he did not know. It was about that time, when he replaced his arrogance with humility, that he rambled into the Ozark Mountains in Missouri, and met up with a passel of "ignorant" old-timers. They talked, and he listened, and thus from them he learned more in one afternoon than he had in three months wandering in the woods. And they made him an Honorary Hillbilly, and dubbed him The Lonesome Hillbilly.

I often write of the city campers and tenderfeet, and often with scorn or condescension. But there is love there, and irony, for I have been there, I was once one of them, and I feel the same scorn and condescension for the youth I once was. I have seen their situation from both sides. What now may seem arrogance is simply experience. The humility is still there, for I still make mistakes, and I still learn. But though I now know a great deal about living in the Wilds, I also know how little that great deal is, not two percent of what there is to know. The little adventures still occur, but the real adventure is the one which that callow youth began, and which continues to this day. It is called Life. The bad things happen, and from them you learn good things, and life becomes better. Assuming you survive. I have counted at least twenty times when I could easily have died, but barely survived, many times from sheer luck. And I also learned that usually I made the luck, from lessons learned in earlier adventures. I strive to pass these lessons on, as the old hillbillies did for me. Sometimes people listen and learn, sometimes they laugh and forget. Those were *my* adventures. You will have your own. You can learn from them, or not. It is *always* up to you. I'm just putting in my two percent's worth.

Aloneness

In most American cultures, "lone" carries connotations of sadness; "lonely" and "lonesome" are taken to mean "by oneself and yearning for company". This is a very bad thing, for it frightens people and bars them from the wonders and joys of being alone sometimes.

"Lone" means "by oneself", "not with others"; no more. No less. "Lonely" and "lonesome" mean "being alone" or "like being alone". A lonely pine is one that stands alone, not near other trees. A lonesome trail is one with no other people on it. There is no sadness implied, nothing bad. Sometimes it is good to share experiences with others, but other times it is better to be alone. Neither is good all the time.

I spend maybe half my time in campgrounds where there are people to talk with and to share with. The rest of the time I am by myself, often out of sight or sound of anything human or man-made. Then I experience what the Scandinavians call Aloneness. I am fully and entirely myself, not influenced by what others expect or think or want or do. There are no obligations or duties laid on me, only those that I make or accept willingly. And, truly, can there be any valid obligations or duties except those that one takes on of his own free will?

But one is also free of companionship, and after a couple of weeks of aloneness, I desire friends with whom I can share. So I go to a campground and make some.

The closest friend is one with whom you can be alone. You can sit together and not say a word, not do anything, not even look at each other. Just be there, thinking your own thoughts, sharing each other's presence. It is enough.

Doing Nothing

It is very hard to do nothing. You can sit by a stream for hours with a hook dangling in the water, waiting for a nibble, but you're fishing. You can sit under a tree looking at the trees and the flowers and the birds, but you're looking. You can stroll through the woods, not going anywhere, just walking, but you're walking *and* looking. Try as you might, you are still doing something.

Most people seem to be infected with a "Do Disease". The worst cases have to actively do at all times. They cannot sit by a stream with a bobber, they have to cast and reel in, over and over. Sure, it is fun and effective, nothing wrong with it, but it is not everything. They never try sitting and waiting. They scoff at it, say it is not really fishing. They hike *to* a place, never just wander with a "gee, what's over there?" attitude. It is as if they are trained to always *do*.

There is a trick to doing nothing: Do not *try*. Do not work at it. Find a very comfortable place to sit, alone, where it is quiet. A breeze is OK, but not a strong wind. Sunlight is fine, but not enough to make you sweat. Sounds are good, but soft ones, not loud or abrupt. No houses or motors, though a train in the distance can make it easier. A softly babbling brook helps. Get comfortable, then relax and enjoy it. You might want to start with your eyes closed, but do not fall asleep. After you get used to it and can just *be* there, keep your eyes open. Do not exactly *look* at anything. See the world around you, but do not put your attention on anything. Hear the sounds, but just let them come; do not pay attention to them.

Do not think about anything. Do not "meditate". Just be there, aware of everything, but *doing* ... nothing.

This is not "Being one with the universe" or "Achieving Nirvana". It is just doing nothing, just being. It can be very rewarding. It is relaxing and calming, and probably good for your health, especially your heart and ulcers. Do not expect great insights into "the Nature of Things". I get peace, calm, tranquility, and just feel good. Maybe you will, too.

Perception

I am always yammering on about looking and seeing, really seeing, what is plain and obvious, all around us, bemoaning the fact that most people do not do it, and are not even aware of their omission. They are not even aware that there could *be* any omission. Sometimes I do not look, I do not see, but I do it intentionally, for there is more, far more, to perceive than is available to your eyes.

Sit, with your eyes closed, and observe. Open your other senses, open them wide. Feel the wind and the sun, and the calm and the shade. Hear the whisper or the roar of the trees Hear the chipmunk skittering through the dust and duff. Smell the living waters of the lake, and the perfume of the pines. When you look at a scene for an hour or more, you see more and more detail. It is much like when you watch the stars: More and more become visible as your sight adapts to the night. So, too, as your ears peer into the landscape, more and more details emerge as your awareness adapts to the plethora of sounds pattering upon you. Breathe through your mouth, to stop hearing your nose. There are leaping fish and singing birds, and chittering chipmunks. Pine cones clack to the rocks, or chunk to the duff. Fishing lures plop with the fish, and reels whine to retrieve them. Children laugh on the farther shore, and a neglected puppy whines for attention. Soft sounds, subtle sounds, constantly there, but rarely heard, because they are *constantly* there. It is the rare and random sounds you normally notice, the sharp sounds that break the background, that intrude upon your attention, like the bark of a firecracker.

Anyone can hear *them*. It is the quiet ones, the ones you have to consciously strive to hear, the ones you must *look* for, that reveal the true richness of the environment. And then the wind comes, and the flood through the trees overwhelms and washes all else away. When the trees talk thus, there is no other sound, and then when they cease, you must start all over, hearing the woods. And that is good, for you get to experience it all afresh.

Now open your nose, and see with it. Concentrate your attention on the airborne aromas. Smell the pines. You cannot help but smell them, they so heavily overwhelm all else. They are like the wind erasing all other sounds, they draw your attention, they insist on your full attention. But you are smarter than that smell, you can set it aside, and perceive others that are equally present, just in less abundance. There is the smell of the lake, which is actually the smell of the shore. Like what landsmen call the smell of the sea, and seamen call the smell of the land, it is the odors of land life drowning in the water's edge, and aquatic life asphyxiating in the muddy beach, and of the mud itself. It is the smell of death, and decay, and rot, and yet it is not unpleasant. Good smells, bad smells, appetizing smells, nauseating smells, these are not inherently so, they are associations, correlations, with pleasure and pain. The smell of a thing that brings pleasure is itself considered pleasant, solely and entirely because we know they bring pleasure. Why, just consider some of the smells that dogs consider attractive. The smell of the shore is a holiday at the beach, and a homecoming after a long voyage. And beyond, or below, the smell of the shore is the scent of the water, the actual scent of the lake. It is not pure. It is lightly touched with fish and algae, all of the abundant life that dwells therein. It is often said of an old fishing guide that he can smell where the fish are. It is taken to mean that he has an esoteric knowledge, the distillation of long experience, whose sum is that he knows where the fish are most likely to be. In plain fact, though, he *can* smell them. He himself may not be aware of it, for the scents are subtle, the differences almost infinitesimal, but nevertheless available to the awareness. Recognition and identification both require experience, but anyone can detect them, if he tries. So you try! First detect, then try to identify. Label, or classify, as far as you can. In time, you will do better, be more accurate. Here is a sweetish smell, a perfume, almost. It smells like . . . like soap. Dish detergent, maybe laundry detergent. Perhaps a camper across the lake is cleaning up after breakfast. Perhaps one of those fishers uses too much laundry soap, trying to get the clothes especially clean. There is a spice, not cinnamon, not paprika, but halfway between. I have never smelt it before. Now a touch of muskiness, like a moose in rut, but there are no moose here, and this is mid-Spring, not their rutting season. Then the wind picks up, twenty five, thirty knots, and the odor of pines washes all else away. And again, that is good, for just as a sip of wine cleans the palate for the next course, so does this aroma wipe away the lingering traces, and leave the nose ready for a new set of perceptions.

The wind pats at your face, and presses your head slightly to and fro, cooling the skin, easing to a sweet caress. It fades away, and the foot not in shade grows warm. You feel the pressure of the log supporting one foot, the texture of the gravel beneath the other. The softness of cotton against your chest, the slightly rougher touch of denim on your legs. The smooth flatness of paper in one hand, smooth roundness of pen in the other The roughness of bark behind your back. The abrupt and shocking thump of a chipmunk leaping on to your leg! And the wind returns to override all else in a sudden full-body massage.

I have written of these perceptions separately, one at a time. I had no choice, for that is how language works, especially written language. I am sorry, but I could do no better. You can, though. Try it. Practice it as I wrote it, exercising one sense at a time. When you have gained a bit of proficiency, combine them. Learn to be aware of all of your senses at once. Open your eyes, and you will see. And hear and feel and smell and taste. All at once. This is what is meant by "mind-expanding". This is what is promised by LSD and peyote. This is what is promised by whiskey and rum and gin. Promised, but not delivered. Perhaps they do allow you to perceive more, but what you perceive is not true, is not what is really there. Open your senses, increase your awareness, and perceive what is there, but that you never noticed, not fully, not anywhere *near* fully Practice this, and your world will become a world of wonder.

You will see.

Summer Sleep

Two of the finest pleasures of camping are steeping oneself in the cool and quiet dimness of first light, and sitting by a fire at night. One lays the foundation of a perfect day, the other adds the final polish. A day with both is magic.

In early April and late September the nights last about twelve hours; there is time to spend three or four hours by the fire, then get plenty of sleep, and still wake comfortably for the dawn. And in winter, when nights are long, you can spend half your waking time by the evening fire, sleep long, then enjoy a morning fire in the crisp dawn, cooking and eating a long, leisurely breakfast.

Those who go camping only in summer miss most of this. Summer camping is wonderful, There is so much to see and to do, weather is usually mild, and the days are long. But the nights are short. If you spend a few hours by the fire, you only have maybe four hours to sleep; most people do not wake till the sun is well up and the cool is gone. Plus they are generally accustomed to a schedule which has them rising at six or seven, often bleary and wishing they could "sleep in". OK, go ahead. The first day or two, snooze. Camping is a vacation, it's for pleasure; indulge yourself. But by the third or fourth day, try rising at dawn. Get to sleep early so you wake with the smallest trace of light. Do it once, and you will surely want to do it again. I often do the evening fire and still rise at dawn after some four hours of sleep, and make up for it with an early afternoon nap under a shady tree. That is another of the finest pleasures, and a tale in itself.

Here is a plan (not the only one) for a perfect day: Rise with the first light. Sit or stroll. Listen to the quiet and to the waking wildlife. Breathe and feel the cool. Have a good breakfast, then spend the morning doing whatever you want. Have lunch. Nap in the grass in the shade of a tree. Go swimming. Do what chores are needed, then cook dinner over a fire. Sit around the fire with your friends. Chat. Relive the day. Watch the stars. Listen to the forest as the fire recedes to embers. Get drowsy as the embers fade. Then sleep, knowing tomorrow will be another, perfect day.

Comfortable Temperatures

When the weather is cool, people dress to keep warm; when it is hot, they dress to keep cool. But usually they go too far, they strive to keep in a narrow range, and this decreases their overall comfort, because their tolerance band stays narrow; a slight change of temperature requires action.

Broaden your range. In the chill of a mountain morning, wear enough to keep from shivering, but no more. There is a point just before shivering where your skin feels sort of tense and the surface muscles are slightly tight. Another half degree of cold and they will shiver, but right now it is okay. Barely. At such a time, think of a very hot day when you would have been glad of the cold, and you will begin to enjoy it, even treasure it. On a hot July afternoon, when the slightest breeze is welcome and you seek even the smallest bit of shade, do not scuttle for the air conditioner or strip down to the skimpiest shorts or bikini. Wear loose clothes, maybe keep them a bit damp, and compare the heat to that of a hot fire on a frigid winter day. The heat will begin to feel welcome.

Whatever the temperature may be, do not fight it. Find something about it to admire and enjoy, something, anything, that you like. Sure, dress to prevent pain or misery. Never try to tolerate frostbite or sunburn. But learn to enjoy the edges just beyond comfort, and your tolerance will grow. You will become comfortable at higher and lower temperatures, you may have less gear to carry, and with less distraction due to fighting the weather, you will have more fun, and more time to enjoy the world.

Communication

One of the most insightful things I ever did was publishing a book. Not writing it. That was a whole different experience.

I write my stories as a personal action, mostly for amusement. I write what I see, what I think, what I *feel*. Then I edit it to make it more clear, more compact. I rearrange the data for a more consistent and logical flow, and to correct grammar and spelling. I add pictures that illustrate the idea or that enhance the mood. I read it a dozen times, polishing it, approaching perfection as best I can. By then, I have the idea cold, and will never forget it.

Publishing is different. I write the stories for me. Then I publish them for you, to share the fun and the insights, to try to make your life and world a bit better, a little more fun. Not for the money; I have enough already. To improve your world, because that improves mine as well.

A book is a communication. I am imparting an idea to you, using ink instead of sound. But I cannot watch you to see that you understand, to ensure that what you heard is what I said, what you understood is what I meant. I have to select words very carefully, and know the difference between, say, "covering" and "blanketing". The difference is subtle, but it does exist. Blanketing is more thorough, more complete, more emphatic. And I have to be careful to not leave openings for interpretation. "Yes, he said one thing, but what he *meant* was something else." No, I never imply, not intentionally. I use the precise word, not its second cousin. I strive to say exactly what I mean, and to mean exactly what I say. But I have very little control over what others think. This is why I despise "political correctness", and scorn those who promote it. "Senior citizen" is vague and inaccurate; "old folks" and "elderly" are precise and accurate, and not synonymous. Think about it.

What, then, is so insightful about publishing? It is the most precise way to communicate an idea short of direct mind-to-mind contact. With the right words, *precise* words, and a few thousand-word pictures, every one carefully selected and polished, I can present an idea clearly and accurately and completely. Of course, the reader can "interpret" it, change it in his own mind, and thus misunderstand it, but listeners can do that, too.

And that is why I write this essay: To communicate to you that what I write is what I mean, as exactly as I can put it into words. "Your self" is not the same as "yourself"; "wonder full" is different from "wonderful".

You would do well to study this and apply it in your own speech. Expand your vocabulary and pick your words with care. Make sure your listener understands what you *meant*; watch for glazed eyes and expressions of confusion. If ever something you hear seems to make no sense, *ask!* Do not say "You're crazy!" Say "I don't get that. Can you rephrase it, or explain it more fully?"

The whole point of talking to someone is (or should be) communication, the exchange of ideas. Many people babble and blather and talk just to be talking. There is no point to their words, and thus they are often repetitive and boring. Make sure your listener is interested. The fact that *you* are interested does not mean that *he* is. A man who has just been told he has cancer is not interested in last night's football game.

Another advantage of publishing is that the author does not get interrupted. Many people much prefer talking over listening. They "listen" to you, but are only waiting for a point where they can butt in and take over the talking, often on a different subject. Often they are listening, but instead of paying attention to what you are saying, they are formulating their own reply. Listen. Understand what is being said. Only interrupt if you do not understand what was said, never to express disagreement. Let the other complete his statement, make his point. *Then*, when it is your turn to talk, express your disagreement. "I see your point, but what I think is..." Or your agreement. "That's true." Then expand on it, or state your viewpoint if details differ.

Cultivate attention span. I know people who will let me talk for only twenty or thirty seconds, then interrupt. If I protest I had not finished, they say "It's my turn to talk", then get upset if I interrupt five minutes later. Wandering attention indicates boredom, which usually results from lack of interest or understanding. TV news gives us fifteen or twenty second "sound bites" so they can change the subject before their viewers realize this "news" is of no importance.

Anything truly worth communicating is worth spending time on, even hours for some things. Pay attention! You never learn new things when you are talking, only when you listen.

And if you do not want to learn something, why are you communicating in the first place?

Cages

Last night in a dream, I saw a room. I had never before seen a room, truly *seen* one, not as I see the desert or the forest or the mountains. As a newborn babe, I did not see the room. The first things I saw were only lights and shadows and things I later learned were shapes, things completely new and strange, unfamiliar, for I had no memory, no memory at all, because in the trauma of death, of losing everything, *every* thing, even my own identity, I had, as almost everyone does, hidden all of my remembrances where I could never find them. There was too much pain in knowing what I had lost. And I hid it so well that now all was new and related to nothing. I did not see the room. I saw - - - I did not know what I saw. After a while, hours, days, eternities, I was taken Outside. I did not know it was Outside, just that the shapes and lights were new and different, changing, but they had always been changing and different, so this was, apparently, normal. In time (and what a long, long time it seemed) I came to understand the difference between Inside and Outside. Inside was bounded, Outside was not. Inside was Rooms, and each room held different Things, and different Occurences happened in different rooms. I came to know and pay attention to the things and the happenings, for they were important. The rooms were simply there, did nothing, only served to separate one set of significant things from another. I never saw the room itself, never *looked* at it.

The years went by, scores of them, and I learned so many things, and failed to learn infinitely more. In time, I learned to look, and to think, and to understand, things that most people rarely even noticed. I returned to the Wilds and learned to look, to perceive, for hours at a time, each minute seeing and perceiving more, more that had always been there, but that I had not noticed. With practice, I perceived more quickly. I gained the ability to see and know in mere seconds or less what had before taken long hours or more. Then, last night, in a dream, I saw a room. I *saw* it. There was nothing in it, vast amounts of nothing. Four walls, painted yellow. A ceiling and a floor. One door and two windows. Light, and air. Nothing else. I saw it as a wolf would see a cage, as a trap, a place of confinement, and as a den, a place of refuge, of safety - - - a place to hide. A place to store things, to protect them from weather and from thieves. And I realized I had never before seen anything so pitiful, so disgusting, so ugly.

A tent is different. It is more a garment, a large coat with big pockets, than a structure or shelter. It will protect from annoyances, from rain and dew and blood-sucking mosquitoes, but not from dangers, from bears or floods or fires. It hardly deters thieves. The air flows through it almost unimpeded, and with two steps, I can doff it. I sometimes do not even put it on, preferring to sleep in the wide open, among the trees and the scintillant stars. Even the blazing full moon is no more than a night-light, and a glowing fire is just as good, a comfort that fades away when slumber curtails its usefulness. I feel no need to hide from the world, for it is my friend, and more, for it is me, and I am the world. We are inseparable. I own it all, in common with everyone and everything else. For though I own it all, so do others. No part is denied, there is no exclusivity. Nothing is locked away where others cannot enjoy it. All is shared, in a commonality bounded only by the fears in small minds, boundaries that only pertain to those same small minds, and are invalid for all others.

I suppose rooms are necessary in cities and towns, where there are so many people that there are always some who are insane, who will steal and destroy and maim by choice. It is a great pity, for rooms tempt one to accumulate properties, and the properties come to own their possessor, and the rooms become so much a part of one's life that one generally becomes uncomfortable without them. I know. I once dwelt in that trap. Even most people I see in the Wilds have brought their room with them, and live inside it, only coming out for a specific purpose, to see a sight or visit a designated "point of interest" or perform a pre-planned activity. I have read of animals raised in captivity and released in the Wilds; their cage is placed in the woods with the door locked open. When the keeper returns to reclaim the cage, the poor confused creature is cowering within, starving and miserable and elated at the human's return.

I will never willingly return to a cage. I may visit one from time to time to see a sight or visit a point of interest or perform an activity, but I will not "live" in one. "No slave can be freed, except he free himself." I cannot free you, but I can point out that the emperor is wearing no clothes. You can scoff and say "You do not understand. You are deluding yourself."

But think about this, really think about it, if you dare: I can say the same thing to you.

Cities Are Your Friends

I like cities. I do not like to be in them, but I am glad they are there. Cities have factories where they make wonderful things such as tents and camp stoves and motorcycles. They have shops that make the parts and materials, all close by so the wonderful things will not cost too much. They have huge stores where I can buy all of the wonderful things in one place. Yes, cities do help to make my life good.

Lots of people live there, too. Mostly they are too timid or weak or ignorant to try a life in the country. Or too greedy, whose only ambition is to accumulate more and more "stuff", foolish people who want "success", but judge success by how much they own. Even some too evil, desiring power, to control other people and tell them what to do. More fear than evil, really; afraid that if they do not control people, the people will hurt them. Cities attract these people, and keep them out of the real world.

There are good and worthwhile people in the cities, too, people who value the comforts and conveniences, and the presence of large numbers of other people. They value these more than they value the beauties and wonders and joys of the wild. I value the opposite, and we are both right. I respect their choice.

I like cities for the things they produce, and for the support they give to their people. I am glad they concentrate these things, and the people, in small places, leaving the rest of the world relatively unburdened. With a very few, mostly minor, exceptions, almost all pollution and overpopulation are in the cities. There is no pollution here, or even litter. There is a family of four in this campground, about a quarter mile that way, and a young couple just drove up and parked their car to go hiking. No over-population here. This is typical of hundreds of campgrounds scattered almost randomly over tens of thousands of square miles of forest, and the population is far less outside of the campgrounds.

I like cities for what they provide to me; city people like them for what cities provide to them. Fair enough. I'll keep the country, and they can keep their cities.

Having Fun

Saturday, early afternoon,and dozens of people are enjoying the lake. My nearest neighbor, two groups, idling on the shore, fishing poles lying unused. A couple of Good Old Boys are passing a joint. Beyond them, a young man fishing from a half-boat, "Fish Cat", it says on the side. He sits at his ease, paddling like a duck with the diving fins on his feet. To the other side are several groups, half a dozen in each, fishing, standing or from chairs, some procuring their dinner, some practicing catch-and-release. A few kids among them. One, a little girl, about four, wields a child-size rod. As I watch, she gets a bite and squeals "Daddy, daddy, daddy-daddy-daddy-daddy!" She reels the fish in, awkwardly, clumsily. Her father dashes over, not ready. "Keep the tip up! Easy! Easy! Keep the tip up!" The fish is drawn closer, closer, he dips the net, and the daughter screams "I caught it!" The intense joy and exuberance radiating from her lights the whole lake and out-shines the sun. Her very first fish, ever! An experience that may be approached, but never equalled, and that will never recur. I have seen it many times, and can never tire of it.

Three women sit in the sun, sipping from cans, chattering while their men cast and reel in, cast and reel in. Across the lake are several more, about one in five fishing, the rest idly watching or playing. Eight or nine kids wander the shore, picking up rocks or rolling them over. Two of them are tossing sticks and stones into the water. One man catches a fish and drops it into a bucket, then washes his hands, thoroughly, and resumes fishing. A boy with one arm in a cast plays with a toy truck, loading rocks in the bed, rolling it ten feet, dumping his cargo, and rolling back for more. Perhaps he is being a building contractor. One lone boy perches atop an eight foot boulder, quietly watching, watching. I know what he is looking at, for he has been there for nearly an hour. He is looking at everything. Everything. He is not bored, he is fascinated. He is *looking,* I am gratified to see him, for he is the coming generation, proof that I am not the last of my kind.

And the dogs lie quietly, content to be with their masters. All except that puppy, who is dashing about from rock to tree to water, amazed that such a place can exist, so different from the front yard.

The park rangers cruise through the campground, smiling benevolently, pleased at the activity, at the people who validate the rangers' work and give it meaning and worth. So many different thijngs these people are doing, each from his own choice, none by the slightest coercion, happy, content, having fun, each enjoying the day as he sees fit. And that is how life should be, in all things, at all times.

O'Havre

I had not planned it. In fact, it had not been a good year for
plans, not at all. I had planned to go to Idaho, then work my
way down through Washington and Oregon and into Nevada,
where I would see The Loneliest Road. It seemed appropriate,
a place I should be.   I would also visit Jarbidge and Lemoille,
places that had been touted to me as well worth my time. Then
I realized I could run the length of US Route 95, something I
had thought of doing for some time, so I replanned the trip.

Immediately thereafter I got chased out of a park because
a wildfire threatened it. I turned this to my advantage by
heading off to Homol'Ovi. I only went there for a couple of
days to be near Meteor Crater, but extended my stay a week. I
doubt I shall ever return to Meteor Crater, but Homol'Ovi shall
be a regular stop. Then I headed north. Well, east and north, to
get on the right track.

But I ran into weather in Kansas, and learned of a unique
map two hundred miles behind me, got captivated by an
intensely peaceful place, and each one shattered my plans anew
and forced me to reassemble them a bit differently. Plans, at
least mine, are rather like a jigsaw puzzle with only a dozen
shapes for the pieces. Any one piece will fit in scores of
spaces, and usually fit the picture very well.

But finally I was doing it, heading north out of Lander,
Wyoming, through Yellowstone to the Idaho Panhandle. Then
my rear tire fell apart, and I had to wait five days to get a new
one. Really, there was not a suitable tire for a hundred miles
around. The folks at Polaris Motorsports called every bike

shop nearby, looking for the tire. Eventually they had to order one. I strongly recommend them to you bikers out there. It is not a Honda shop, but they went out of their way to get me back on the road, and did not overcharge me for the service. Fortunately, if you must be stuck somewhere for almost a week, Lander is a great place to do it. If you are ever in the vicinity, find a reason to get stuck.

So I was a week late on my current itinerary. I headed north, and a bit west, pushing myself. Forced marches, as it were, getting all of the distance I could each day, to catch up on my timetable. But I never made it to Idaho. The Northwest was burning, Mother Nature forcing payback for a century of interference, a hundred years of arrogant two-legs not letting the forests burn. Well, they were burning now. See, my plans are not the only ones to go wrong. I never saw the fires, but the smoke was thick, and kept getting thicker with every mile I advanced. It was too much. I could smell it everywhere, I could feel it in my throat and lungs, I could see it all of the time. Photographs just would not turn out right. Oh, sure, they were nice and artsy, like soft focus and those lovely Japanese landscapes. But that was not what I needed. Finally I faced the facts, and abandoned my Northwest plans; I would just have to do them another year. Which is a good excuse for some future trip, not that I need any such justification.

I turned around, and discovered Falls Campground in the Bridger-Teton National Forest. It is only about sixty miles from Lander, but a good bit higher elevation. And I fell in love. It is beautiful country, high montane, filled with firs. It is going to burn heavily one of these years, as it has been hit pretty hard by the pine-borer blight, but is still magnificent. And the skies! High and dark, far from any significant light pollution, if it had not been for the smoke, it would have been perfect. In terms of dark, it was Bortle Class One every night, but the smoke acted as a high haze; no shadows from the Milky Way, and the fainter stars were obscured. And then the wind changed and the smoke dissipated for a week. I may be back next year. Yes, definitely next year. I know of no darker skies in the United States.

Now, I could happily spend a couple of extra months in southern Wyoming and Utah; that had been my intent since turning back. But there was another problem: The aspens were turning, and it was only early September. The deer and the elk and even the squirrels were changing color and looking ragged and shaggy from growing their winter coats early. Bears were gorging, birds were beginning to migrate. Fuzzy caterpillars were fuzzier than they usually were. The temperatures had been warmer than average, but were starting to drop. It was not a certainty, for weather never is, but it sure looked like an early winter, and probably a severe one, was already on its way. The local old-timers and Indians agreed.

So there I was, heading south. Now, the only decent routes through Utah or Colorado passed through some pretty high passes, passes that could quickly become impassable with a single blizzard. I have seen snow in July, and given the signs, would not be surprised at being forced to take to the eastern Colorado plains to reach the South. But not for the next week, at least. I was on the central route, just east of Vail, and across the Great Divide through Hoosier Pass, 11,539 feet. Downhill, a long way. I cut the motor and coasted for more than four miles. My destination was the Four Mile Campground near Fairplay. That lies about halfway to Sugarite Canyon State Park in New Mexico, where I planned to stay at least a week, and get my bike some standard maintenance. R&D Honda in Raton, another excellent bike shop, indeed, one of the best I have known. But the turn to Four Mile said it was eight miles up. Likely mostly dirt road, I figured, which I prefer to avoid with a trailer. I knew another campground, Buffalo Crossing, was not too far south, so I changed my plan and headed for it.

Well, that plan did not pan out, either. The turnoff is not well marked, or at least not prominently enough, because I missed it. I pulled over, consulted my maps. I could go back, retrace my route. I do not care for doing that. A bit farther on, maybe twenty-five miles, the map listed another campground, O'Havre Lake. It looked like it was not more than four miles from the highway, and every mile was a mile closer to Sugarite, so on I went. It was easy to find, well marked, but the road immediately turned to gravel. I *hate* gravel roads! I would much prefer bare dirt! The only thing worse is deep dry sand. But the road was smooth and well-maintained, no ruts or washboarding, it was getting late, and I was almost out of the forest, so this was really my last chance. I took it.

Two miles in, on a passable road, I came to the notice board. It had a sketch map showing where it was, and where the campground was. Looked like maybe another half mile up a side road. This one was not gravel, not steep, and wound a bit up the mountainside. But after a quarter mile, it went through a series of switchbacks. The inside curve was deeply rutted, old ruts, smoothed by much traffic, but still deep. Now, this is one of the worst things for a trailer, especially behind a motorcycle. One wheel drops through a ten-inch deep hole while the other stays level. This jerks the tongue to one side, which jerks the bike, and tries to throw it down. This while moving slowly to negotiate a hairpin turn, on a road with a distinct sideways slope to a thirty-degree dropoff. Followed a couple of hundred feet later by another one. And another. And another. There must have been twenty all told, each one worse than the last. If the first switchback had been in the condition of the last one, I would have turned back and camped dispersed for the night. But it was not, and it lead me on, and eventually, I made it to the top, four miles and a bit from the highway. A few hundred yards of smooth and fairly straight road, and I was (at last!) in the campground.

Now, you have read enough fiction to know the routine. You know how these long and difficult struggles to reach a place invariably turn out to be well worth the trouble, for the destination is a paradise, is as close to perfect as any place can possibly be. And here was O'Havre Lake Campground, and it was not. Perfect, that is. In fact, I would have to say it was mediocre. Plenty of trees, but not enough space between sites. Drinking water, toilets, fire rings and no fire ban. But very little firewood, having been well picked over by a great many campers. The lake was maybe an eighth the size of Morphy Lake, which is pretty durn small. It was very reminiscent of Maverick in Cimarron Canyon. Pretty full, too. Three open sites out of about thirty. On a Wednesday in mid-September. The fishing *must* be great, or else these Colorado people have mighty low standards. Then again, it lies at over nine thousand feet, so it never gets too hot. And it is about one hundred fifty miles from Denver, only a three or four hour drive, and the dirt road in, while almost a nightmare for a motorcycle, is not too bad for a car, even with a trailer. You might bottom out once or twice, but you will get there. Still, I doubt I shall ever return.

Morning I dreaded. I had to negotiate those switchbacks again, but downhill this time. Just like hiking, riding downhill is more difficult than uphill. Especially with a trailer. One that has no brakes. I had a little experience with such adventure, notably at Morphy Lake, but this would be the first prolonged ride. Almost two miles of rutted switchbacks on which I dared not go over the edge; I would drop the bike first, as a last-ditch tactic. I figured forty minutes, maybe an hour, to negotiate the entire road.

When I first had this sort of experience with a trailer, it took me by surprise. My second at Morphy Lake, was much more severe, and I was glad of the first event. I recall think the first one was Trailer 101, and Morphy was 201. I also feared there might be a Trailer 301 coming up. Well, here it was. Fortunately, it was not so bad. The first two courses prepared me adequately. Sure, I had to make the turns at only one or two miles per hour, but the straight stretches were pretty good. I had not noticed that on the way up, having most of my attention on the worst parts. Typically human; we notice and pay attention to the bad things, and almost have to concentrate to include the good. I reached the highway in only twenty minutes. There I stopped and had a smoke and a rest.

The remainder of the trip was quite nice. Today I was not fighting a headwind, as I had done pretty much all of the way the day before. Traffic was very light, and the scenery was usually sort of breathtaking. At least until I got out of the mountains and on to the Colorado foothill plains. In fact, my mileage was half again what I had gotten all of the previous day. And eventually I reached Sugarite Canyon. I pulled into the Alice Lake Campground, and found there were only three sites not occupied, and all three were reserved. Even the overflow was filled to capacity. On Thursday, mind you, in mid-September. It would appear I was not the only one fleeing an early winter.

However, one of those reservations was mine. I *had* planned that.

A Dirty Job

Life on the Road is not all fun and games. There are things that must be done; there is no way, or no practical way, to avoid it. Like packing up when leaving a camp. You could abandon your gear, and buy new stuff near your destination. I did see some people who did just that. They flew in from New York or Boston, bought a full set of equipment in Utah, and spent two weeks at Bryce Canyon National Park. On the day they left, they simply threw away all of their gear. I do not know, maybe it was cheaper than shipping it all cross-country (twice) and storing it for a year. But it offended me, even though I got one of their chairs.

One such job is truly dirty, and the main reason I do not live life as if each day would be my last. You do, too. If you *knew* this was to be your last day, would *you* do the laundry? Not that I do it that often. Denim shirts and jeans can be worn for a week or more, if you do not sweat much or crawl around in the dirt; three of each can last a month or more, especially if you often wear short pants (which last even longer) and no shirt. Socks, T-shirts, underwear, they can easily be washed by hand, so you do not really need many. Why, washing them is hardly more than washing your hands, and gets that done at the same time. So, laundry ten or twelve times or so a year is enough. But still more than I like.

Still, most laundromats now have free wifi, so I can check my e-mail and play around on the Web. Usually. This one has no wifi, so I am sitting here bitching about laundry. But there are a lot of things I would rather be doing.

Washing dishes is another dirty job. Sometimes in the low desert, they have to be washed twice; you have to get the dust of before you can use them. Hauling trash away also has to be done. I minimize it by not generating much in the first place, and by burning as much as I can, but there are still a few bits to get rid of.

Some dirty jobs, though, are a pleasure, can even be fun. Bathing, for example. Mostly it is swimming, but even a sponge bath is pleasant, because it feels so good. A hot shower is a sybaritic joy. Now and then, I will even get a motel room, just so I can have a long, hot soak in a tub. When you only get it once or twice a year, when you *cannot* have one any other time, a hot soak becomes almost infinitely valuable. And yet, for many years I could have had a tub soak any day, even twice a day, and only took showers. And never missed the soak. Old Will was right: "Man is a giddy thing".

Gathering firewood and cutting it up is another thing I find fun. Of course, you have to know how to do it right, how to be efficient about it, but I do, so it is fun. Also good excercise, and *much* more pleasant than calisthenics. It is almost a stroll in the park. For me, it is a walk in the woods, since I almost always gather a bit of wood on the way back.

Even when on permanent vacation, there are things one must do, regardless of druthers. The trick is to do them as efficiently as possible, and to find something, however small, to like about them. Washing dishes means my fried rice will not taste of chile. Or dust. Washing clothes means my clothes will not itch, and (usually) I can play on the Internet for an hour. Gathering and cutting firewood means I get a to have a fun campfire on a chilly morning.

It is all in your attitude.

Wampum

When I was in school, we were taught how the white man had constantly ripped off the Indians by trading cheap goods for valuable properties. The classic example is twenty four dollars worth of beads and some whiskey for Manhatten Island. It sounds to us like a pretty massive cheat, but let us look at it in perspective. In the seventeenth century, a dollar was a lot of money. Two or three dollars per week was pretty good wages, so twenty four dollars then was roughly equivalent to $4500 or $5000 today. It is still a very low price, thirty or forty cents per acre, so the whites made quite a profit. On the other hand, the Indians did, too. Beads today are cheap. They cost, very roughly, about forty dollars for enough to make one square foot of beadwork. $5000 worth would be around 125 square feet, or over three and a half million beads. Back then, beads probably cost fifty times as much to manufacture, so figure the Indians got around seventy thousand beads, maybe two and a half square feet. But the Indians made theirs by hand, carving them from rocks, shells, horn and bone, or baking them as tubes of clay rolled around a grass stem. If it took ten minutes to make one bead, that would set the cost at over a dollar per bead. So figure the beads received were worth $70,000 to $100,000 to the Indians.

My teachers were very condescending about the innocent and gullible red man accepting such a pittance for so much valuable land. Well, the land was not that valuable to the Indian. They had no use for a seaport, so Manhatten was just another bit of hunting ground, and not a particularly good one.

Plus, the beads were not cheap trade goods to them. Beads, loose or woven into a cloth, were wampum. Wampum was universally accepted among all tribes as money. It *was* money. Coinage. It had a great deal of inherent value, and was not easy to come by. If you want to be condescending about a money system, take a look at gold. What is so valuable about gold? It is very useful in electronics and in dentistry, but not irreplaceable. It makes lovely jewelry and decoration. And that is about it. In the mid-seventies, gold sold for $140 per ounce. Today it is bouncing around $1200 per ounce. Because it is more useful? Because it is less common? Because the dollar is worth less? No, only because people *say* it is expensive. It has "treasure value". Take that away, and gold would probably drop to less than $100 per ounce. Wampum, on the other hand, has *real* value. Little bits of clay, rock or metal, or (most commonly) of horn, bone or shell. Tiny bit. Worked into a roughly spherical shape, usually, with a hole bored through it. Try making some. Shape a bit of seashell, then bore a hole through it, using no power tools. It is a lot of work, and the result is one (count it) *one* bead. Just the labor, today, would cost at least a dollar *per bead*. Add cost of materials, wear on tools, storage, transportation, profit for the trader, and you double or triple the cost, at least. They are now getting Manhatten for eighty dollars an acre. Minimum.

Cloth woven from beads is even more expensive. I do a bit of beadwork, decorating my clothes, making hatbands and headbands. With modern tools and materials, it takes, on average, about eight minutes to do one 1" row of beads. That does not include designing the work and setting up the loom, just selecting beads and threading them on a needle, then weaving them into the cloth. At twelve rows per inch, that is 96 minutes per running inch. Five inches in an eight-hour day.

A twenty two inch long hatband one inch wide would take over thirty-five hours, or four and a half days. Double the time to account for design, setup and tucking in the threads when done, and you have nine days, seventy-two hours, or $720 at ten dollars an hour. Just for labor. It requires 4,896 beads, or $4,896 at one dollar per bead (the cost for the Indians; more like ten dollars at today's values). Double that to account for profit, transport, overhead, and we are talking $10,000 in a two foot belt ($1,500 today). You can see that wampum made a pretty good medium of exchange, good money. It was actually worth something, all by itself. It cannot be counterfeited. It is durable, and can stand a lot of handling. It is compact and lightweight and useful.

The Europeans did cheat the Indians in many cases, but Manhatten Island was not one of them. From the Indian's viewpoint, it was a very good deal. It was, though, still a rip-off, since the Indians who sold the island did not own it in the first place.

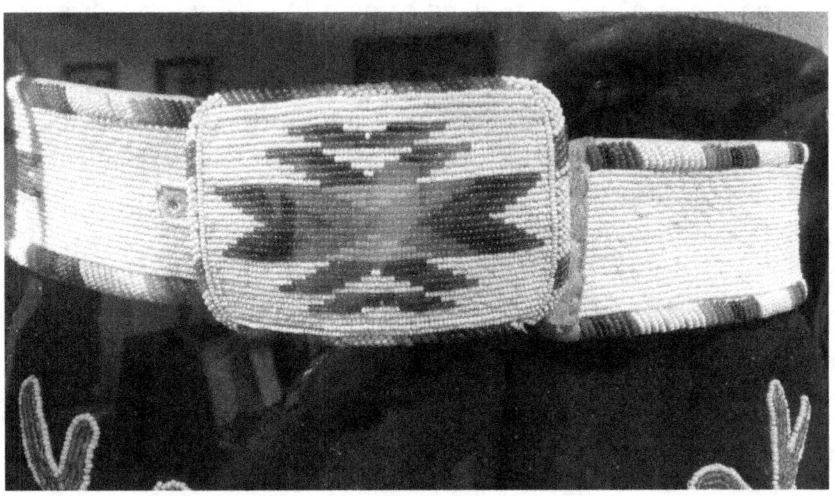

The Micron Mind

I am thoroughly astonished. I never found such a thing before, and if I had ever anticipated the discovery, I would never, never have expected it to manifest here. New York City, perhaps, or Hong Kong, but not here! "Here", by the way, is up in the Monzano Mountains. Hills, really, covered by a forest of short pines and tall junipers. Here is where you expect to find people who appreciate the esthetics of nature, the non-human values of the world. Why she came here, I do not know. Certainly she has the right, but why would she ever *want* to?

She has a keen sense of value; she can look at a thing and deduce or calculate its worth almost instantly. But to her, "value" had only one meaning, one sense: Practical value, and strictly from the commercial viewpoint. What *use* is a thing, or can be made of it? This land around this campground is not very fertile, it cannot grow viable crops or serve as pasturage. It can grow trees, slowly. So its only value is as a source of timber. And the unit of measure of practical value is the dollar. Trees grow slowly here, and are difficult to remove once cut, so the profit margin is low. Therefore the land has small value. The beauty means nothing. The ecosystem is immaterial. The wildlife that thrives here is of no matter. The vegetation holds the land in place, keeps it from eroding, and allows a decent aquifer to exist, and that maintains water flow which is used for irrigation. So the plants do have a use. But other than lumber and water, the land is a waste of space. It would not even make a decent parking lot.

The legal definition of the value of a thing is what that thing will bring, how much money one can get for it. To her, the sole value of a work of art is how much it will sell for. This painting, to her, is better than that one, because this one cost ten thousand dollars, and the other only cost five. The subject of the painting, the skill of the artist, the concept communicated, all are of no importance. Just the price tag. I am surprised that she is "camping" (she is in a fully-equipped motor home), but even more so that she is in a state park that charges fourteen dollars per night. There is an RV park near here which charges thirty. Wouldn't she rather be there? I asked her as a satirical joke. She missed it completely. Yes, she said, she would, it would obviously be better. But the man she was with chose this spot.

It is amazing, and also a bit frightening, that such people exist, with minds so narrow. If I accused her of being unable to see the beauty here, she would deny it. She can see the beauty, but an equal-sized parking lot would be much more beautiful, because you can charge people four dollars an hour to park in it. I do not mind that she has such an attitude; pity it, perhaps, but not *mind*. What scares me is that so many people are intolerant, and wish to enforce their values and their viewpoints on others. If she was such a person, with her values, and had the power to enforce them, campgrounds such as this would not exist, or if they did, would charge much more, as much as they could, because their sole purpose (to her) would be the amount of profit they could generate.

Profit is a good thing. Fair profit. But there is so much more to life, so much that is more valuable, more worthwhile, than mere profit. The legal definition of value reveals a lot about our culture. It is contaminated, poisoned, with the idea that money is the only standard of value. Money is one of the *least* sensible standards of value. (I think I just lost most of my audience, there.) Money is useful, very useful, but when it becomes the standard, beauty, esthetics, get pushed aside. In my opinion, there is nothing as valuable, as desirable, as beauty, esthetics. Now, if we could come up with a beauty standard to replace the gold standard, and base money on that . . . It may not be practical, but it certainly would be valuable!

Zippers

I experience no end of fascination in seeing how the obvious can escape people for so long, even in the face of evidence shouting, screaming for attention.

The latest example is zippers. Wonderfully useful things, zippers. They are most commonly used today in clothing. Short ones, maybe six or eight inches, for the most part. It used to be that the fly of a man's pants was held closed by buttons. I have had such pants: Levi's Button-Fly Blue Jeans. I liked them for the retro feel, sort of a rebellion, though I did not realize it at the time. I just thought I was being cool. One more example of how we can lie to ourselves. In actual fact, the buttons were not nearly as good as zippers; they were more complicated to handle, took longer to close, and the button-holes wore out. Zippers were quick, easy, and almost never broke or wore out. In almost every case, the zipper was still functioning perfectly when the fabric was reduced to three sets of patches. Of course, these are the original design brass zippers. They are still made, and likely always will be, because they *work*, and work well.

For some people, though, that is not enough. There is a more recent design, the coil zipper. It is made of plastic, and is much cheaper. Items made with coil zippers are cheaper than those made with the original brass type, and thus can be sold for less, and that, to a great many people, is more important than durability. Sleeping bags are a good example. I always get the Coleman Montauk model. I have used dozens of bags, and the Montauk suits my needs best. When it is too hot, I just lie on top. As it gets colder, I use one as a blanket, then zip it and crawl inside, then use a second one as a blanket on top of the bag. If it should get really cold, say, down around zero (Fahrenheit), I can tuck one inside the other and zip them both; I have not needed to do that for some years, as I strive to avoid temperature extremes. I can also zip them together into one big bag for, shall we say, social occasions. The only problem is the zippers. The bags themselves do not wear out. They do not fray or tear or develop holes. They do not compress and thus lose their insulating properties. They do not tear out their stitching, which would allow the fill to shift and leave empty gaps between bunches of fill. No, it is the zippers, always the zippers, that fail. Once the zipper stitching came loose, but that was easy to fix. But when the coils go, it is another story. They wear down and no longer hold. In the middle of the night, you roll over, putting lateral pressure on the zipper, and it pops open. Then you have to get out of the bag and painfully work the slider down till the zipper is completely open, and close it up from the beginning. In the cold. And by the time you are done, the bag has lost all of its heat, and you have to shiver for ten or fifteen minutes while the bag warms up again. And when the zipper has popped once, it is much more likely to pop again. Four or five times, and it simply will not work any longer. Now your sleeping bag is only a thick comforter. It is a very *good* comforter, but if it will not zip, it is not a sleeping bag, and it is far less effective at keeping your body warm. Your only viable options are to replace the zipper, or get a new bag. Sewing sixteen feet of seam is a lot of work, so I just head for the nearest Wal-Mart. A new bag will usually last me about a year, which is not bad, when you look at it as three hundred and sixty uses. It only costs forty dollars, so it works out to eleven cents per night. I end up using each bag as a bag for a year, then as a comforter for another year. When I buy a third bag, I throw away the first one. (Incidentally, unzip the bag completely before washing it, else the inside will not be cleaned well. Also, the agitation of the washing will strain the zipper and probably ruin it.)

Tents have much the same problem. Back when I used plastic dome tents, the door zipper was always the first thing to go. It was not a big problem, unless I was in an area infested with mosquitos. I could always use a couple of safety pins if I wanted the door closed; drafts were not a problem, because dome tents are *designed* to be drafty. Excuse me: To always have good air circulation. Much the same thing. I usually *like* drafts. And the failure of the zipper generally happened near the time the fabric was wearing out. The plastic breaks down under UV light, and in high altitudes and wide-open deserts, you get a lot of UV. Eight or nine months of daily usage is about the best you can expect from these tents, which probably justifies using the cheap coil zippers instead of solid brass-toothed ones.

All of this became moot when I finally decided to make a canvas tent. It would have a zipper for the door, because you have to have a zipper; that is how it is done. But I would use a good, solid, reliable, long-lasting heavy-duty brass-toothed zipper, and never have any problems with them ever again. Right. I believe I have mentioned, somewhere or other, that I learn something new every day. It is quite humbling to realize that no matter how much I know, how much I learn, there is always more, and more, and *more*, still unknown. Not to mention what I know that turns out to be wrong. I studied tents. I learned all I could find about designs and stresses and what could be expected of the materials. Then I designed the tent to incorporate all of this data, and be the best tent I could concieve. With a brass zipper. Not buttons or ties that would leave gaps to allow mosquitos and no-see-ums entry. Zipper. Continuous. No gaps.

I made the tent, and it was good. It had two big windows for ventilation, with curtains to keep rain out and to allow them to be closed against wind or sight, and mosquito netting held in place with velcro, for easy repair and to keep the edges tightly sealed. Pitched with taut guy-ropes, it was neat and orderly and looked very, very good. Professional. But the taut ropes meant taut fabric, and taut fabric meant sideways strain on the zipper, and that, when the strain was coming from strong gusty winds, meant the zipper fabric, the cloth to which the brass teeth are attached, began to fail. I had to redesign the door to have a couple of inches of slack when the tent was pitched, and replace the zipper. (A bit of luck helped out here; I needed a twelve-foot zipper, and the shortest I could find that was at least twelve feet was forty-five feet long. That is enough to replace the whole zipper twice.) But having the slack in the door meant the door side of the seam would be longer than the jamb side, so I had to lengthen the jamb, and that meant the zipper would not be quite smooth; it would be sort of wavy on the jamb side. Not hard to accomplish, but it made the slider difficult to move. And the front of the tent had to be pitched *just so*, to avoid putting any side strain on the zipper. If there was side strain, if you pulled the slider in just the wrong way, the teeth popped apart behind the slider. No disaster, no permanent damage such as occurs with coil zippers. But it does mean you have to run the slider all of the way to the end of the twelve-foot length and off of the teeth (and you do this with both sliders, of course), then put the sliders back on, one on each end. Not hard, not difficult, does not take a long time, when done in full daylight, at your leisure. But it is at best inconvenient, if you have to do it when you want to go to bed. When it is dark, so you have to position a flashlight just so, and need both hands to manipulate the zipper and slider. And it is probably cold. Maybe raining. With gusty winds jerking on the fabric which you are trying to hold still. But it must be done. And you have to have a zipper, at least if you want the tent to be bug-proof.

It is fascinating, how the obvious can escape people for so long. Remember the windows? With mosquito netting? Held in place by velcro?

It took two days to replace the zipper with velcro, and it has never given me any trouble since. Most of the time was taken up by recutting and hemming the door, taking out most of the (unsightly) slack I had added. It is quick and easy to close up, if you leave the last few inches for the middle of a long straight stretch, where pressure from just one side is sufficient to complete the seal. It is even quicker and easier to open. Replacement, should it ever be needed, will only take a couple of hours. And it is even more rainproof than the zipper.

Honestly, it is obvious. Once you have thought of it.

Independence

Well, here we are coming up on Independence Day, and most of us are getting ready to celebrate it. Not all, unfortunately, for one couple has just cut short their vacation and abandoned their plans. The furnace in their RV broke down. They were okay at night, bundled up together in their bed, but when morning came, they could not get up. Sure, it is July, but at eighty-five hundred feet, that just means snow is less likely. There was frost that morning, and my friends could not cope with it without their furnace. The camp host told them of an RV shop some thirty miles away, but I do not see that it will help; the city is down at four thousand feet, where it is twenty or thirty degrees warmer. Don't need no furnace when it ain't cold, so why fix it? (Sorry, hillbilly ethic.)

Independence.   Do you really know what it means? Independence Day celebrates our newborn nation becoming free of the parent country. Actually, what it celebrates is our declaration of freedom; actual independence did not come for several more years. We had to fight for it, first, till Britain gave us up as not worth fighting for. But there is a lot more than that to independence: It means not being dependant, and is far more than a mere political situation. Independence means not having anything you *depend* on, that you have to have, for which you have no substitute or alternative. My friends are dependent on their furnace. They could have lighted their propane stove, maybe placed a cast iron pan on it to help radiate heat, but they either did not think of it or did not consider it workable.

Independence is not an absolute, like pregnant or dead. Their are degrees of independence. I am not dependant on my trailer; if I lost it, I could still travel. I would have to abandon half of my gear, but more than half is easily dispensable. My bike, on the other hand, I do require. At least, *a* bike. I could not live year round backpacking, as I lack the youthful vigor it requires. So I am careful to take good care of her, servicing and maintaining her as needed.

It is an important thing, out here, to be aware of what you truly need, what you are dependant on. Then you can make plans on what to do should you lose or break an essential item. My hunting knife, for example; I carry a spare. Means of making fire; I have six or eight lighters, and half a dozen other firemakers. Spices? No backup needed. Camp stove? Much food does not need cooking. Weather radio? Not essential. Pots and pans? I can cook without them. Find a good book on basic backpacking; it will list what the bare essentials really are. If you have the proper training, you can survive anywhere in the American wilderness with nothing more than a knife. *That* is independence.

But it is uncomfortable, and dangerous. To be happy, I need someone to talk to, to share with, at least part of the time. I need my sleeping bag and tent, so I do not spend half of my time finding or making shelter. I need books and a flute for esthetics. I have a cot, and tools for making things of leather, cloth, wood, beads. I have a computer and e-book reader, for writing, videos, music. They are tools, comforts, things to make life easier and more fun, They are good to have, but not vital, not necessary. The trick to not being owned by your possessions is to be able to do without them, to be willing, if necessary, to abandon everything. Then you can enjoy them, and do as you please.

You see, there is a balance between liberty and security. In general, the more liberty you have, the less security, and vice-versa. Medieval serfs had little liberty; they were bound to the land, and could not leave their farm without express permission from their baron. On the other hand, they had security; they could not be expelled from their land unless they committed a major crime such as murder. We have many laws, far *too* many laws, to provide us with safety and security. Look at just about any law or rule or regulation. You will find it deprives you of a liberty. It says you are not *allowed* to do something. In most states, you are not allowed to ride in car without wearing a seat belt. Bad law. That is not to say that wearing a seat belt is a bad idea. Making it mandatory is a bad idea. It should be left to individual choice. "It is for your own good" is the same as saying "you are not smart enough to watch out for yourself". Requiring children to wear seat belts is a good law; they are dependant on their parents, and do not have the option of making the choice for themselves.

A few laws, a very few, are needful. The rest simply increase one's dependence on the government. Likewise, a few items of equipment are needful in the Wilds, most of the rest are only for comfort or convenience. Many are downright destructive to the camping experience. Satellite TV, for example. If you live on the Road full time, television is not so bad, but if you are only out for a week, you are wasting time with it. You could be sitting around a campfire telling tales. Is your favorite show so important? Is your imagination so retarded that you cannot dream in the flames? Have you seen the stars so much that they no longer interest you? I have little respect, and much pity, for people who "camp" in a fifty foot motor home or trailer. (Again, full-timers are a different breed.) They are utterly dependent on their gadgets and gimmicks, their luxuries and life-enhancers. They literally cannot live without them. Even when they come out here, they cannot seem to enjoy the forests and streams and mountains and deserts. They will look at them for a short time, maybe hike for an hour, perhaps spend the day driving through them and stopping at Points of Interest and Scenic Views. Really, they might almost as well stay home and watch a documentary.

To appreciate the Wilds and get the most out of your camping trip, you need to leave behind as much of your "stuff" as possible; it gets in the way, and prevents you from seeing the Wilds. Bring only what you need. Make a clean break from your accustomed day-to-day existence. That is what vacations are for. Break your dependence on can't-live-without garbage and experience a completely different world. Absorb it. Let it absorb you. Sit and look at a meadow and see how much, how many details, you can notice. All you need is a chair, and a comfortable seat against a rock or tree will do just as well. Get away from requirements and regimentation and now-you-are-supposed-to.

I live in a country where one can do this. That is what we are about to celebrate.

Nature

Beauty

Most people go camping to experience the beauty of the Wilds, the Great Outdoors, untrammeled, unspoiled Nature. But they carry with them their preconceptions of what they are going to see, and often are bitterly disappointed when reality does not conform to their expectations. In the past week I have seen more than a dozen parties arrive at this campground only to leave the next day because Nature has let them down. They expected to find their dream of Beauty, and were confronted with a wasteland. Or so they said, in their blindness.

This campground was once heavily forested, with dozens of mature trees, most more than a century old. It was shaded and cool, with rampant squirrels and resplendent birds. Then came the blight, the pine borer infestation. The trees died, and were felled and hauled away, leaving a bare field with only an occasional Colorado Pinyon or Limber Pine. Now, a few years later, there are some aspen, four or five feet tall, and a few pine seedlings, none over three feet, averaging about thirty feet apart. The beauty seekers look at it, groan, and hurriedly depart. Three or four of us stay for a few days. My plan had been to stop over for two days, but I immediately changed it to a full week.

Why? Because it is so beautiful! A field covered with green and yellow grass, and liberally blended with a myriad of flowers of a score of species. Red, orange, yellow, blue, purple. Daisies and goldenrod and imperial thistles as much as four feet tall. Evergreen shrubs like a bonsai forest, infant pinyons only inches tall, chipmunks and ground squirrels dashing about, sparrows and robins pecking and poking, and all moving in concert with the intermittent Wyoming wind.

At the edge of the campground, where the dead trees still stand, a tall snag spreads long limbs silhouetted against the sky. Although it is pine, its spread is reminiscent of an oak after dropping all of its leaves, slumbering through the Winter. But this is the Summer, and you can see, you can sense somehow that all life is gone. It is a beautiful corpse.

Beauty is said to be in the eye of the beholder, but it lies really in the mind. The brainwashed camper comes to visit the forest to see beauty, because trees equal beauty, and therefor no trees equals no beauty. He does not stay. Ironically, he could walk a hundred yards southwest, and there he would find himself in a grove of lodgepole and ponderosa pines miraculously missed by the borers. Or he could walk a hundred yards northeast, into a small hollow of lush undergrowth in swampy soil, split by a noisy brook that is lined with thickets of willow. I like to stroll to the North in the cool mornings, then sit by the stream in the hot afternoons. If it weren't for the wanderlust, I could stay right here for a month, absorbing the pure art of the real world.

To appreciate the Wilds, you must have an open mind. Forget travel brochures and Hollywood special effects; they are not real. Stop, step out of your vehicle, clear your mind, and open your eyes. *Look* at the world, *see* what is here. Accept it as what it is, not what you expect or want, or *think* you want. It will not fit in any mold, it does not care what you desire, it is what it is. It is all beautiful, but you have to look, really look, to see it. A glance is rarely enough; it takes time. And the longer you look, the more you will see, and the more beauty will unfold before your awestruck eyes. Beauty is always and only in your mind. It feeds upon what you sense, and grows as it is fed. Nurture it, and give it time, and it will reward you, beyond your dreams.

Size

I am sitting on the east rim of a deep and beautiful mountain valley, almost a canyon. Far to my right I can see where it begins. At first it runs straight towards me, then it curves by me feet and continues curving till, twice as far to my left, I again look straight down it as it breaks from the mountain side into a much broader and gentler valley. This one is not gentle. It starts so, emerging from a thick grove of juniper, the slope of its sides barely discernable, but the angle rapidly grows ever steeper; by the time the valley reaches my vantage point, the slopes lie at forty-five degrees, and they continue to steepen to sixty or seventy. In some places, half of the wall is vertical. The sides, especially upstream, are mostly heavily cloaked in juniper, with grasses and other mountain undergrowth between. There are a few trees of other sorts scattered about, mostly ponderosa pine, but a tenth of them live oak. In some spots, the bare dirt lies exposed, peppered with broken rock. Starting about where I sit, outcroppings of bedrock protrude, creating terraces to trap loose soil and provide beds for the montane flora. Greedy plants! Some are so determined, they do not wait for a provided bed, but sprout directly from cracks half-way up the vertical cliff! The very bottom is lined with shattered rock, water-tumbled and washed clean. Tiny critters crawling among them look like ants. There is no river or stream, or if there is, it is what we term intermittent, no water at all that I can see, but clearly it holds a raging torrent when there is enough rain. It is that torrent which carved the valley.

I stand on the rim and gaze down, into the depths, feeling that perverse, suicidal urge to hurl myself off. On the far side, one of the valley's denizens frolics playfully along the bedrock edge, jumping casually from rock to rock. He is having so much fun, I can no longer resist. The urge grows, and grows, and with a sudden surge, I leap off the rim!

Four bounds bring me to the bottom, startling the frolicing chipmunk, who darts into a hole. Well, yes, the valley *is* only twelve feet deep here, and a bit over twenty feet wide. But it does get deeper! It is over twice as deep at the far end, twenty-five, maybe thirty feet! What, you thought it was, like, the Grand Canyon? Yes, the juniper cloak is the ground variety that rarely grows over eighteen inches tall. Yes, there are only ten trees on the northern half, nine ponderosas and one live oak. Yes, the bedrock outcrops are only two or three feet tall. No, I did not use a cliche in describing the ant-like critters among the rocks; they look like ants because they *are* ants. So what? This valley has exactly the same features as one a mile wide, just not as many of them. It has just as much beauty per square foot, and it has some wonders that the larger valleys can never have. Here are a couple of giant trees towering twice as tall as the valley is wide. Show me *that* in the Shenandoah!

It is wonderful, down here in the valley, cool and shady, calm and peaceful. Wildflowers stand among the bracken and brush. A breeze funneled up the valley brushes away the bugs and flies. Chipmuks and red squirrels, emboldened by my lack of motion (for a brought a chair with me), sport about the rubble and duff, chipping seeds from pinecones and squirreling them away in their holes. Miniscule mice cautiously cower in crevices and timidly venture forth, wary and ever watchful of the gigantic chipmunks competing for the same foods. These normally nocturnal varmints feel much safer here, and they are.

These jumbled boulders, only eight or twelve inches long, are fresh and new. They have not been long tumbled by steadily flowing waters, so their edges are straight and sharp, not smooth and rounded. They offer hundreds of hiding places, nooks and crannies and random passages and tunnels that no predator can predict. It would take a wise and patient wolf to winkle a mouse from such a place, and a very hungry one as well, to risk the bruises and scrapes inevitable among the unstable and shifting stones. No, the little folk feel much safer here, at least, when I sit still.

The valley lies along the edge of Rueter Campground, right next to site fourteen, as close as Owen Creek is to my beloved Site Seven. I call this Fourteen Valley. But most visitors never see it All they see is that there is a gully in their way. They do not see the gully itself, just that it is there. They do not see the chipminks and squirrels and mice; they barely see the trees! They are looking for deer and elk and other large animals, and they think they have to cross the meadow on the other side and hike through the hills to see anything. It is ironic. Their noise and motion make it much less likely that any animal will stick around to be seen, and the poor hikers get all hot and sweaty and scratched up in their fruitless search. I can sit quietly on the rim of Fourteen Valley, in soft, cool, breezy shade, and watch the teeming population scampering among the stones, and at the same time see a dozen or so deer, especially does with their fawns, and sometimes an elk or two, browsing through the meadow on the far side. You want to see wildlife? Look for the little ones. They are far, far more numerous, very much more active, and so vastly more entertaining than watching a lone deer nibble, take a few steps, nibble again, over and over. I have seen bison herds, a hundred or more, being watched by enthralled tourists (a hundred or more), snapping photos, oohing and aahing. And what were the bison doing? Same as the deer: nibble, step, nibble, step. They do not have much of an act. Maybe the tourists are waiting for the bison to charge. Now *that* would be exciting! Squirrels and chipmunks perform all sorts of amusing antics, then sit up and stare at you, begging for food. "If you think we're funny," they say, "you ought to pay, you know."

I am reminded of an old cartoon I once saw, of two tourists excitedly gaping and pointing at a balancing rock. You know the type: An ovoid of stone perched upon a pert bedrock pedestal, carved loose by eroding sand and wind and ice, but still balanced in place. Only the rock in the cartoon was just three inches tall. Actually, this little one should be *more* amazing than a ten-footer, because it would take so much less force to dislodge it. But no, it has to be big, and the larger it is, the more people will gasp and wonder over it. They will not deign to even notice the little things.

No, my friends, size does *not* matter. Once you realize that, more than ninety percent of the world, a part you did not even know existed, will open up before you.

You are welcome.

White Sound

The name of the river does not matter, nor does its location. That this spot lies ten miles from the Continental Divide has some small importance, for it means the river is still in the mountains, and it is fairly steep, and it is teeming with rocks. But if it were a thousand miles from its source, it would make no difference, so long as the bed was as steep and as littered, and the water flow as broken and battered, as full of foam and random obstructions, disruptions, distortions. Even the time is of no importance, for dusk or dawn, morning, noon and night, light or dark, hot or cold, the river still runs as it runs, and as the first rivers ran, and all rivers since, and all that are yet to be. Geologically, it is timeless. Time can be told by sun or stars, but not by the river. Time means almost nothing Only in the depths of Winter, when the cold is so intense that the river is silenced, covered completely by a solid surface of ice, and the early Spring, when the hills' snow-cladding melts and raises the river to exuberantly sing its joy as the birds do to greet the dawn, burying the banks, washing the leaves and litter from the riparian rocks, only then is the Voice of the River raised or covered, as is the river itself.

About two hundred yards from my camp lies The Road, a highway, but a small one, paved here, but soon fading into dirt, to wander on to the lands of a wilderness area. It lies at the wall of a canyon, of cliffs that refuse to crumble, and rocks that weakened and fell, of gravel and sand that once were staunch and steadfast bedrock. The Road sits on a high bar, what was once the bed of the river, an ice age or two ago. It is just high enough that I can see no sign of it, not even the seldom traffic that pursues its path. Even the sands cannot be perceived from this position, for my camp is made a mere twenty yards from the current bed of the river. It is not so much that the sounds of the river overcome those of the road, it is more that the soft riversong accepts the intruder, absorbs it as harmonies, and they become as one.

It is a special sound, and yet generic. It is all frequencies and all values, all tones and pitches and timbres, all present all of the time, changing constantly and unpredictably in moment-to-moment detail, and always the same. It is so constant and ever-present that one often forgets to hear it. As beams of all colors of light blend to become white light, so do all forms of sound blend into what we call white noise.

It is the Voice of the River, the fabled White Sound. It has many dialects, many regional accents, from the dull booming roar of heavy surf playing the shoreline like a giant drum, to the spring shower making a harpsichord of a mountain pond. There are words and meanings buried in the sounds, which have spawned many religions, with shamans who interpreted the messages just as Greek and Roman priests interpreted the drugged mutterings of the Oracle at Delphi, or some modern preachers interpret the "speaking in tongues" of ecstatic and frenzied worshippers.

And the messages are there. They truly are. If you were to take all of the music ever written, great and good and bad and horrible, and perform them all together; if you were to gather all of the speeches and orations, all of the diatribes and sermons and exhortations ever declaimed by Man, and speak them all at once; if you were to take all of the peals of laughter and shouts of joy, and all of the screams of pain and cries of panic, and voice them all in one outpouring of emotion; then you would hear the Voice of the River.

It is a joke which the Universe plays upon us. All Truth, all Meaning, can be heard in the watersound, just as all great and small speeches can be found in the dictionary, and the winning lottery numbers found in the list of One through Fifty. The Truth is there, but also so much nonsense that it is easier to pan the gold dust from the sands than it is to learn facts from the water. At least you can recognize the gold when you see it.

So what is the use, what is the good of the river's rambling, aside from the esthetic? Though one could argue that the esthetic is enough, there is more. If you abandon your inhibitions and unfetter your imagination, then *listen* to the water, there is no telling what ideas may be brought forth. For the most part, they are only entertaining, like the images we see in clouds, but deeper thoughts, concepts of practical value, may also emerge. The trick is in distinguishing the one from the other. They lie in you, buried by beliefs and lies and wrong assumptions that have deluged us all of our lives. The water-sound can free us of distractions just as it eliminates highway noises from my camp. And just as a single word or phrase may trigger a thought or a memory, so might the river's voice, for all sounds, all words and phrases, are contained in it.

But even if you have no interest in such philosophical concepts, even if you are certain that all spiritual questions of any consequence have all been answered, even if you think this is all used hay in a cow pasture, there is still the sound, the pure sound. It is restful and relaxing, calm and cool, a lullaby that can sooth away all cares and concerns, for a while. If you will let it. It is a lullaby, the first and oldest of all lullabies, ever. It is white music.

Infant Mortality

Most people believe that advances in science and medicine have extended the human lifespan, but they have not. People talk of the folks in the middle ages mostly dying by the age of thirty, and of forty years old being the equivalent of a modern age of ninety, The truth is, the maximum lifespan was about the same as today. Many people reached one hundred years Not as many as today, but we have a lot more people now. No, the benefits that science, largely through medicine, but mostly through agriculture, have given is lower infant and child mortality. In the old days, the majority of children born died before puberty, most of them in their first or second year, of disease and malnutrition. This dragged the average, what we call Life Expectancy, down several decades, say to about forty. Add in the brutality of the times, the greater chance of being murdered by bandits or soldiers, the lower quality of medical care in many (not all) places, and the much greater risk of malnutrition or starvation from crop failures and the inability to ship large amounts of food more than a few miles, and Life Expectancy dropped to about thirty. (The exact figures may be a bit different, but not by much, except in a few isolated localities; not by as much as a decade.) But once a person had survived to adulthood, the chances of living to seventy (three score years and ten) was, in many places and times, about as good as it is today.

Nature is far behind us in this respect. The only medicines the wild animals have are a few herbs that some of them know to seek out when they have an upset stomach or a fever or a wound, and agriculture is almost unknown, with exceptions such as ants who raise aphids or fungus, or octopus who plant oyster beds near their dens. All of the rest are hunter-gatherers, entirely dependent on finding what they need. Some, such as squirrels and woodpeckers, will store food for winter use. Most simply gorge themselves when food is plentiful, building reserves of fat against times of scarcity. Bears eat ravenously when they emerge from hibernation, because they are literally starving, but then eat rather leisurely (but still greedily) through Spring and Summer. In the Fall they gorge frantically, packing away every calories they can get their tongues on, building up their fat for winter. Sort of like lazy people, putting things off till the last minute. I used to procrastinate like that, but I never can seem to get around to it these days.

Because of this lack of control and planning, infant and child mortality in the wilds is, among mammals and birds, much like that of human barbaric cultures. Among the reptiles and fish and especially insects, they are tremendously greater. Each female fish lays hundreds or thousands of eggs, yet only a few, perhaps two or three, survive to breed another generation And among plants, mortality is mind-boggling. A great fir produces a thousand cones, each bearing a hundred seeds. Many cones are plundered by squirrels before they ripen. Most of the seeds that do fall are found and gobbled by birds. Many of the remainder fail to germinate. Still, the tiny seedlings sprout thickly, sometimes a dozen or more in a single square yard. Most of them die, from lack of water or nutrients, or roots too small and shallow to survive the freezing Winter, before they are three feet tall. Those that do survive will crowd each other, competing for the vital sunlight, with only the strongest and most fortunately placed succeeding. And when the wildfire comes, as it always does, all of the recent seedlings disappear as puffs of smoke, and most of the saplings are seared too badly to survive. Only the few who are large enough to survive the scorching, the mature elders, and a few youths who were not too close to the flames, remain after the conflagration among the charcoal and ashes of their weaker brethren. And over the centuries and millenia, the total population of trees remains much the same.

Often a new species will arise that avoids the normal infant mortality and expands to out-grow and out-compete the other life forms that want the same resources. Look at grasses. A few tens of millions of years ago, there were no grasses at all. Then the first one showed up, proved massively successful, and split into scores of species. Now there are grasses in almost every environment on Earth. Man came along and figured out how to cultivate some of the grasses for their seeds, changed his diet to include more grass seed (wheat, maize, rice, barley, oats, rye, etc.) than everything else put together, and now man is almost as ubiquitous as grass. And there is the Viet-Namese jungle fowl that *used* infant mortality; it made itself tasty to humans, and easy to raise, submitted to our domestication, and now, as the chicken, is more populous than the humans themselves. Granted, their infant mortality is worse than ever, especially in the United States, since we eat almost all of the eggs they lay, but as long as Man is around, Chicken will never become extinct.

Infant mortality affects species, too. How many species evolve, but die out in just a few generations? Even fail to have a second generation? "Concerned" eco-simps promote the myth that on average one species becomes extinct every day. They do not know that they are quoting a made-up factoid from the second *Jurassic Park* science fiction novel (it is in the introduction, along with more false data and wildly incorrect arithmetic).   But what they never seem to consider is the question of how many new species evolve each year? *We* do not know, we *cannot* know, especially among the insects. We have not even finished classifying them.   I wonder if any biologist has ever looked into this.   It should be good for several doctoral theses.

There must be trillions of intelligent races in the Universe; after all, the place is just so darn big! Every single race must go through a life cycle, from barbarous infancy to civilized childhood to wise maturity.   Most die before maturing, and never get off of their native planets. We will have to do that, get into space where there are infinite resources, where we can build little worldlets, each supporting thousands or millions of people (along with our symbiotic animals and plants). Perhaps leave Earth as a protected park, a wilderness area, a nest which we have left behind, but still like to visit. Perhaps even a womb where another sentient race can develop. We can do it. It is possible.

But infant mortality of species is so high! We had best get a move on, while we still can.

It Just Happened!

I have not yet found it, but someday I will. Somewhere, perhaps in northern Illinois, perhaps in a valley in the vicinity of San Francisco, or maybe even in a barren and desolate canyon in a Nevada wilderness, somewhere it must be, and I will find it. Perhaps there are trees, from which they are picked. Perhaps there are flocks of them, herds in the hidden places, where the new ones are born. I am open to any possibility, which is why I know I will find it, the source, the place from whence the wild computers come.

There are people who tell me computers were invented by men, that they have been deliberately designed and manually manufactured. I find that absurd. For all I know, they develop in the rocks, growing from native minerals just as crystals form from quartz. These Human Supremicists, these materialist pseudo-philosophers point out the intricate complexity of the circuitboards, point out the dozen specialized components that work together perfectly, that *must* work together perfectly, else nothing would work at all. They ask if such a thing could happen by chance and accident, and seem utterly baffled by any insistence that they could. I am baffled by their persistence in insisting they *have* to be man-made. Are the trees man-made? The flowers? Man himself? Look at a human body, even at a single human cell. Are these not more intricate than any computer? Did they not happen and evolve by sheer chance over hundreds of millions of years? If these complex conglomerations of cells "just happened", why, then, could not a computer "just happen"?

Okay, enough satire. I know that computers are built by humans. I have built several myself. I know they do not form spontaneously; it just does not happen. I also look at complex ecosystems, from soil to microbes to plants and animals. I look at DNA. I look at the human eye. The shamans tell me these things evolved through the workings of random chance over millions of years. I look again at the human eye. Each part, lens, retina, iris, is useless by itself. Each one is a major step in evolution, each dependent on all of the others. There are no existing examples of gradual development (which evolution requires), because gradual development could not occur; if it did, there would be several generations of creatures with non-functional eyes. Several major changes would have to occur at the same time, and each would have to occur correctly, else the eye would not work. It would require fantastic co-incidence. (I will admit that such a fantastic coincidence, while unlikely, is not impossible.) And it would have to have happened more than once. The eye of the octopus is almost identical with the mammalian eye, but it is clearly on a completely different evolutionary path. The mollusc and mammal paths diverged long before the complex eye existed.

Someone designed these living things. Could be a god, could be a massive team of technicians, could be just about anything. I do not know. Whoever it was, it has my respect and admiration. It was not a perfect job; there are many obvious improvements possible. But it works, and has worked for millions of years, at least, and shows no sign of breaking down. The manner in which eco-systems adapt to changes in climate and other conditions is truly amazing. Even more amazing than the gullibility of people who think we can significantly disrupt the system for more than a few years.

Life and Death

The desert is a deadly land. The alpine glaciers and naked crags may approach it, but only approach, for while any life which enters will more likely be killed than not, little enters, so little dies. The desert, though, abounds in life, almost as much, in numbers if not in mass, as a tropical jungle. Go ahead and laugh, it is good for you. When you are through, come take a look at reality.

The desert is full of life. There are no thousand year old giants towering four hunded feet in the air. Here the thousand year old giants may reach the height of a man. Or not. Jungles teem. Teeming implies motion, the frenetic rush-hour scamble of an anthill, or the silent roar of a maggot encrusted carcass. Deserts do not teem. They are still, and silent. Dust devils speed across the sands, but nothing else does. A roadrunner may race a hundred yards. A rabbit or a ground squirrel may dash a rod or two. Lizards may zip as much as three feet. All the rest is lazy, leisurely, refusing to exert in the broiling, baking heat. Hawks, buzzards, vultures, glide in effortless circles up where the air is some twenty degrees cooler (a mere hundred instead of a hundred twenty). The little creatures cower in shadows, for at ground level in the direct sun, the temperature may exceed a hundred forty, the point where rare roast beef is done. The desert is a deadly land.

When the weather is dry, as it almost always is, with a bare three inches of annual rainfall, the gray weathered plants sleep.

Don't they look peaceful?

Don't they look natural?

Don't they look dead?

The entire landscape is almost nothing but black, gray, brown and tan. Only cactus, some of them, are entirely green. Cottonwood green is half gray. Palo verde green is half brown.

And then it rains. The plants awake to frantic action, storing sunlight, engaging in orgies of reproduction while they can. They sprout, grow, blossom, seed, die. A few days, a week at most, when the desert is dotted with color, green leaves and wildflowers  of every hue, tiny, for they have no time to grow larger, and little water from which to build cells. They leap out, fire off their seeds, then duck back under cover. They spread leaves, build and store sugars till they run out of moisture, then huddle underground till the next capricious rainfall. Unless...

Sometimes, some very rare times, there comes a deluge, several years worth of water, all at once, in a single day, or maybe two, and broad areas, acres, even square miles, lie submerged for a time, a brief time, but long enough for much of the water to soak into the ground, beyond the reach of the sun, beyond the risk of rapid evaporation, where it will feed the flora for months or more. And if the year is wet, a rainfall every month or even more often, then does the desert show its hidden potential. Then does the desert, the whole gray desert, bloom. It turns green.

First come the expected desert wildflowers, the ones that adapted and evolved to bloom and seed in mere days. Then, as the moistness persists, the newer immigrants begin to emerge: dandelions, thistles, chervil, burdock, mullein and milkweed. Natives of foreign climes, tired and poor wanderers from the crowded woods, from huddled masses in the foothills and the meadows that lie hundreds of miles away, sprouting from seeds tempest-tossed on the winds or traveling steerage in the guts of birds, air-dropped from a thousand feet above the golden sands. Foreigners hoping to build a new life in a distant land suddenly turned clement. And among the weeds and herbs appears the grass. Grass! Trademark of the prairies, it does not belong in the desert! Who ever heard of a grassy desert? But as the weeks go by, and the rains continue, rains at a rate that would be called sparse anywhere else, but here is sheer abundance,

the grass grows longer, and spreads. The whole plain turns green. Where did all of these seeds come from? Have they been accumulating for years, decades, more? Hiding among the rocks, hoping to win a rain lottery? Evading the notice of frighteningly efficient birds and rodents? However they have done it, they have succeded. They have done their duty and fulfilled their promise, they have found work, and can finally write home.

And now, here, on a mid-winter day that looks like spring in kinder lands, in the midst of life appearing from nowhere, where no one would expect it, where few would even believe it possible, the desert shows just how deadly it is. Clusters of broken branches, ghastly gray fingers reaching from the grave, sprout burgeoning masses of leaves, bright green, dark green, with tinges of yellow and flowers of blue. Twigs that seemed dead admit they had only been kidding, hiding amongst the mummies of their less fortunate friends. In some rare clumps, every branch is clothed, every limb is alive. In others several sticks remain gray, unresponsive to the liquid largesse, flatlined from too long a delay before the arrival of aid. And some of the bushes remain entirely gray, beyond hope, thoroughly, completely, utterly dead.

Here stand trees that have lost half, three-quarters of their branches. Trunks withered and broken, shed their bark, and only one, maybe two branches bear leaves, still in possession of the spark, the essence of life.

And many stand yet unchanged, stark against the green, slowly decaying, returning to the dust. Here are life and death, coarsely mingled together. Green and gray. Future and past. Hope and despair. The desert is a deadly land.

The rains continue, for a while. The land may become lush, if the weather pattern persists for a year, or two, or more. But one day it will cease. One day the rain will no longer fall. One day the precipitation rate will fall back, and the desert will again have to make do with its accustomed three inches per year. And the grass will shrivel, and the dandelions die. The greasewood will grow gray. The leaves will fall, and crumble to dust, and the dust will blow away. The prolific bugs and birds and beasts will diminish in proportion to their dwindling food supply, and the coyotes will grow thin. And life will disappear, the few survivors hiding in the scorched shrubs as the relentless sun again sears the sands. For the land is still a desert, and the desert is a deadly land.

But the trees will remember. Their thickened rings will remain, record of the wonderfully wet times. And the creosote, larger and thicker than before, will shelter the tiny creatures a bit better, for a while. At least, until the less lucky limbs eventually succumb and finally fall away. And the roots of the grass will hold the sand, resisting erosion, for a while, till in time, they, too, weaken and fail, and become one with the dust.

The dryness of the desert will kill such a vast abundance of life. But it will also preserve the store of seeds, billions of potential lives laid down to wait, by parents who laid down their own lives for their descendants. And in time, next year, next decade, next century, the desert will again grow wet, and the life it has preserved will return and grow, and prosper for a time. For the wheel must turn, and even though the desert is a deadly land, before a thing can die, it must first live. The desert will see to that, as well.

Transition

The world is gray, and bare. Thin, scraggly overcast dims the light. A few junipers, some stubborn cedars, are green, grayish green, and a few clumps of weed lend a bit of color, even some purple premature flowers. But even these few traces of life seem dusty, old, somehow tired. The land is grave, and barren. The trees are thick with spindly twigs, forlorn sticks lacking any leaves save for a few brown and withered remnants that neglected to fall with their brothers. The only lives apparant are clusters of mistletoe, and even they are more yellow and brown than green. There is no vigor. There is no growth. There is no joy.

Regardless, I pitch my tent among the naked trunks, next to a line of saplings, meager six-footers, apparant failures, void of promise. Almost. One of them, a bit more eager than the others, precocious, impetuous, impatient, has managed, for no discernable reason, to anticipate the change, to precede the incipient burgeoning of Life. For it is coming, as surely as the seasons. In fact, *exactly* as the seasons. The lone sapling, still lacking the slightest leaf, has thrown forth a dozen blossoms. They are a clarion call, an invitation, a challenge, a declaration: Winter is *over.* It is time for *Spring!*

And it is time. It is magical. The dead gray sticks take on a slight green tinge, which daily grows, stronger, greener, more dominant, till the traces and smudges gather and assume the shapes, wedges and oblongs and distorted circles, of leaves. As useless and unproductive as new-born babes, they yet bear the shape of maturity, and the same inherent potential for infinite achievement and creation that also lies dormant in the baby. Day by day they grow, and more of their like sprout beside them. One tree still shows no growth in its lowest branches, but there are buds on the next rank, and more, and larger, increasing as they approach the peak, where there are not only new leaves, but new twigs, young branches already a foot long, reaching, straining higher and ever higher, pulling at the rest of the plant as if striving to take to the air. It is the personification of Spring, from gray and bare to gravid and bearing, new life arising from old death, hope from despair, abundance from destitution, wealth from poverty. The flowering sapling throws forth leaves, and her sluggard sisters begin to bud. The brown sands magically turn green, as roots buried in dust send up shoots and blades of glowing green grass. A majestic fifty-foot cottonwood bursts forth in green, leaves that burgeon and swell, so swiftly one can almost see them grow. Each day the world is visibly greener, dull brown and gray giving way to brightness and color. The heat and energy of life warms the air, and the trees sway and fan the clouds away, attracting more and more sunlight, so much that the day is not long enough to hold it all, and the hours of darkness dwindle and diminish before the pressure of expanding light. Sparrows flock to the newly clothed limbs, seeking sheltered sites for their new nests, out of reach of the snakes, out of sight of the raptors, safe havens for the nestlings soon to come. Rabbits move more freely, ranging boldly (for rabbits) now that longer grass and ceilinged brush offer concealment and camouflage. Tiny insects begin to stir, warmed from doped dormancy, exposing themselves before ravenous robins, yet managing to breed faster than they are browsed. Moths emerge from chrysalis and cocoon to flit through the dusk and the clement evenings, pollinating and propogating. New seeds begin to form in the grasses and weeds, a new harvest that will be ripe when the birds most need it to nourish their insatiable young. Daily the winds lessen, gusting storms softening to gentle zephyrs reluctant to disturb the new leaves, or daunted by the solid-seeming masses which the leaf-clothed trees have become.

Winter strikes back, unwilling to depart, but the blows are too feeble, their impact too weak. A day or two may be cooler, but the effort cannot be sustained, and the warmth returns, greater than before. The dawn may still grow cold, but the morning moisture no longer freezes; there is soft dew, but never brittle frost. The morning campfire loses half of its charm, for it can no longer provide the intense pleasure of warming numbed hands; the numbness no longer comes, and the heat now supplies only delight, and not deliverance. The morning sun is still greeted with outstretched arms, and it is greeted with relish, but not with relief. Not any longer.

It has been a good Winter, pleasant in its own way, a time of repair and replenishment. It has been a time of sharing with old friends, sharing stories of the past, and good times of the present, and dreams of the future, and the simple presence of each other forever. It has been a time of relating finished travels, and of anticipating new ones. But it is over, at last. The Road is calling, and the anticipation can now become experience. The snows are leaving the mountains, the heat is investing the deserts, and the cool is rising slowly to higher altitudes. I will follow the cool, and experience this time of rebirth and renewal, over and over, as I rise in altitude with the rising warmth. I will make this enchanting first week of Spring last for two months, or more. I can do that. I know the spell.

So mote it be!

The Stump

We are going to hold a seance. Join hands with the book, left side in your left hand, right side in your right, look at the picture, and concentrate. Call upon the spirit of the ancient tree, picture it in your mind as a hundred foot healthy adult, and ask it for any messages it may have for us.

In 1814, the last battle of the War of 1812 was fought, a couple of months after the war ended. At the same time, a very enormously lucky Ponderosa Pine seed sprouted in the high mountains of western Wyoming. Just sprouting was pretty lucky in itself; most such seeds are eaten by birds or squirrels, or just rot in the ground. This one became a seedling. Then, because there was enough water and nothing stepped on it, it grew into a sapling, but slowly. After all, it stood at over nine thousand feet above sea level. Sacagawea and her followers Lewis and Clark had already passed through the area, but Jim Bridger was trapping in the vicinity, and may have seen it. He would not have noticed it, though, a mere seedling just three or four feet tall. Just as most people would not have noticed little Jimmy Bridger when he was only three feet tall. About the time the Alamo became immortal and the Republic of Texas won its independence, the sapling was still less than two inches in diameter. It had been fortunate to survive this long because no fires had seared the patch of ground it called home, but as this would certainly happen, sooner or later, the youngster began to thicken its bark to protect the living cells from intense heat, and to drop its lower branches so a ground fire could find no path to the green upper limbs. Texas joined the Union, then

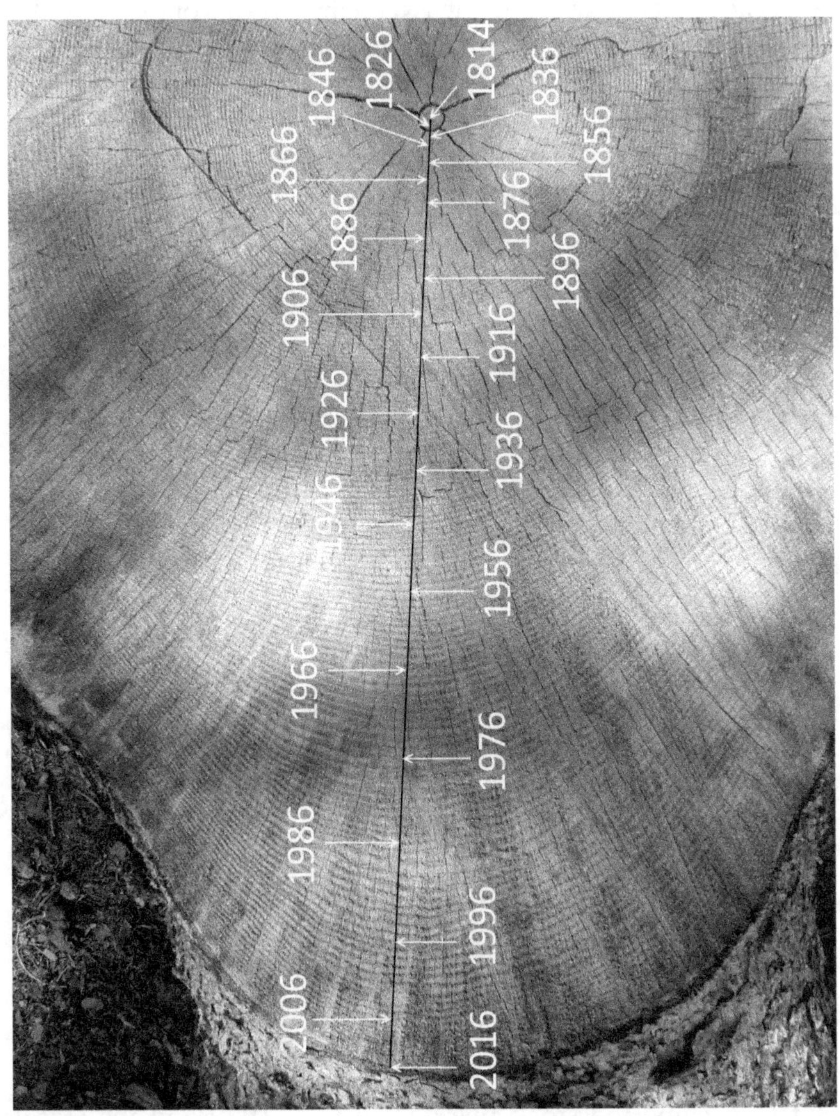

1814
1826
1836
1846
1856
1866
1876
1886
1896
1906
1916
1926
1936
1946
1956
1966
1976
1986
1996
2006
2016

seceded along with ten other states, and was brought back in. A decade later, our nation was celebrating its one hundredth birthday. By this time, the sapling had become a young tree, six inches thick. The tree was now mature, at least enough to survive the flames when a wildfire did sweep the forest, close enough to have killed a younger tree. Many thousands of other seeds, those that had germinated around the time this one did, had died from one or another of the many, *very* many, threats and hazards that beset the infant trees, the saplings, even the young adults. But quite a few others of its age-group had also survived, as well.

The tree had been lucky, but it was not finished needing good fortune to survive. It was mature, but still small. It still had many trees of its generation competing for water and sunlight, and many elders, well and firmly established, and taking, by seniority, a large portion of the resources available. The climate had been benign all of its life, with rainfall well above the centuries-long averages. But now, about the tree's sixtieth year, the climate changed. The rainfall diminished, became less and less each year. The tree continued to grow, but like the rainfall upon which it depended, less and less each year. Fortunately, the tree now had fairly deep roots, and could seek old water, and no longer be completely dependent on what little fell and seeped into the soil.

For thirty years the rain was scarce. The automobile became practical, and heavier than air flight was achieved. World War One began, and the trenches in France were deluged by the heaviest rains in living memory. The French blamed it on the cannon fire, but they were probably mistaken, for in western Wyoming, the rains had also returned, and our tree flourished and grew through two decades of abundant rainfall. But then came the stock market crash of 1929 and the Great

Depression, and along with it began the Great Drought in the mountains. Boulder Dam was built, and the TVA electrified Tennessee. Movies became Talkies, and radio brought news and entertainment to every part of the country. World War Two ended the Depression, but not the drought. But no sooner had the War ended than, for no discernable reason, the rain returned in abundance, and for ten more years the tree grew faster than ever before, even as television was swiftly superceding radio.

By now it was one of the Elders, two feet thick, stable, respected, a pillar of the forest, utterly immune to any but the worst of fires. Most of the other elders were of its own generation, few as much as twice its age. It grew while it could, perhaps making up for the prior dry years, perhaps in anticipation of drought yet to come. For come it did. Before Sputnik took the world by surprise, the Great Drought had resumed, and growth slowed. What growth there was was mostly concentrated in the great buttressing roots, perhaps because they were the sources of most of the water gleaned from the drying soil, from the diminishing water table. For sixty years, while computers entered the civilian world, then became household appliances, and spawned the Internet and cell phones, GPS and digital cameras, the tree persisted, ever growing, impervious to almost every possible danger. 9/11 went unnoticed, and 2012, the year the world did not end. No rival tree could shade it out or steal away its water. No fire managed to penetrate its thick armoring bark. No animal could gnaw through its immense trunk. Even lightning could only damage it, not kill it, for it was too big. A lightning bolt could explode its top or shatter a limb, even rip a long scar down its flank, but such things a tree can survive. But here the trees enormous luck finally ran out, for there was one danger, a tiny little beetle, the Pine Borer, against which it had no defense.

Swarms of the bugs infested this stately giant, perforated its fireproof bark, cut the internal tubes which transported vital water to the energy gathering needles far above the ground. It withered and died, brought down by an almost invisible insect.

Well, not quite brought down; Man did that. The tree stood in the middle of a developed campground. It was still living, but many of the limbs were dead. The Rangers feared that, in falling, the great branches might injure campers. This was considered to be not a good thing, so the decision was made to cut the tree. In 2016, in the tree's two hundred second year, it was felled. The faller was skilled, and made a smooth and uniform cut, leaving the stump clean and easily read, at least, by those who knew how.

"What stories would these trees tell," the poet wrote, "if trees could speak?" As you have seen, they can speak, and they do tell marvelous stories. If you first learn the language they use, they can spin yarns that would make Homer jealous.

And they can even speak from beyond the grave.

The Great Quest

Aside from air and land, there is probably nothing so much unappreciated as water. It is taken for granted, and few people ever think much about it, if at all.

I am sitting by a lively brook, watching the water play with the rocks and tickle the fish, leaping barriers and outsmarting dams as it relentlessly pursues an inexorable trek to the sea. There is a drop of water flowing past, a Wandering Droplet, which rose, months or years ago, from the Pacific Ocean, evaporating into the sky, riding the winds to the east. It flew over the coast, dodged between mountains which drove its less fortunate cousins high, too high. Icarus fell because of too much heat; the water falls because of too little, condensing into heavy drops which fall and shatter on the rocks below, then merge and slip lower, always lower, to form springs and tiny rills, brooks, rivers, and eventually drop, like Icarus, into the sea, there to rest, then evaporate and try again.

Our drop is wiser, more experienced, or just plain luckier. It stays low, as did Daedalus, and does not fall. Farther east it soars, wandering a bit north, a bit south, but always east. Many, most, of its cousins fall, but it persists. Persists, at least, till its luck runs out. One peak too many, one updraft too strong, and it, too, condenses and falls, splattering on the ground below. But it did not fail, for it had crossed the Great Divide. Though it no longer flies, at least it flows east. Like a salmon in reverse, it seeks its place of birth.

Not directly east. It has fallen in the Big Horn Mountains of Wyoming. The stream flows west, but will soon turn north and join with other flows, making its way to the Missouri, the Mississippi, the Gulf of Mexico. Eventually it will join the Gulf Stream and cross the Atlantic Ocean.

It will take much time. There may be delays and detours. It may evaporate from a Western river and ride the winds for a while. It may be drunk and carried far in the body of a mouse, then of the hawk that eats the mouse. It may be drawn into a sapling and be part of its tissues for two hundred years before the tree dies and rots, releasing our drop to continue the quest. But time is nothing. Eventually, it will reach the sea.

On the far side of the Atlantic, perhaps after several long circuits around the Big Pond, the drop will again take to the air. It may be a fog in London, or a drizzle in Berlin, or even a flurry in Moscow. It will join rivers, flow east or west, perhaps as far as the Black Sea, then south to the Mediterranean, and back to the Atlantic. But it is persistent, our tiny drop, and sooner or later, perhaps evaporating from the Caspian Sea, it will drift just far enough east, and debouch into the far Indian Ocean. From there, the Quest is sure. Flowing with the ocean currents, soaring on the winds, the drop will find its way to the Western Pacific, and ride thousands of miles north and east, to glorious Success, to Honor, to Recognition as World Traveler, Circumnavigator of the Globe!

And then? Why, quietly evaporate and do it all again. And, who knows? Perhaps, in hundreds, or thousands, or millions of years, The Wandering Droplet, on a day just like this, may flow past this very spot again. And possibly, just possibly, I may be sitting right here watching it.

Man and Nature

Man and Nature

Why do people distinguish between Man and Nature? Why the pretended dichotomy between "man-made" and "natural"? What is the difference between a beaver-made dam and a man-made dam? Size, perhaps. Materials, sometimes. I doubt that any beaver, any sane one, at least, would ever consider building on Man's scale, but I can easily imagine a rapt beaver gazing respectfully at the Grand Coulee Dam and thinking, "Two-Legs do have their faults, but they sure can build dams!' Beavers build dams for their purposes, quite cleverly, and humans build dams for theirs. What is the difference?

Humans build cities with residences, stores, factories, hospitals, warehouses. Ants build nests, underground cities, with the same things. No real difference. Prairie dog burrows serve the exact same purpose as human burroughs. Humans domesticate sheep and raise crops. Ants domesticate aphids and raise fungus. Humans build roads, animals make trails. Humans fight wars; so do ants, chimps and wolves. What do humans do that non-human animals do not? The only real difference I can see is a relative one: Humans make and do things for human purposes, the wild things make and do for their purposes. Thus the correct dichotomy would be Wild and Tame. Tame is defined as altered to suit our purposes. Thus Grand Coulee Dam is tame, and a beaver dam is wild. From the beaver's viewpoint, Grand Coulee is wild and the beaver dam is tame.

Humans are smarter. Some of them. Potentially. Maybe. Coyotes can distinguish between a man with a stick and a man with a rifle. Ravens know how to open a velcro pocket and a zipper. Turkeys know to look left and right before crossing a road. I watched a dog use a tennis-ball thrower to play fetch. I have seen squirrels train humans to throw food.

Humans are spiritual. The sane ones are aware that we are a part of a great machine, a massive self-balancing eco-system. Sometimes we are very destructive, abusing a section beyond recovery; usually we take what we need without doing undue damage. Un-natural? Grazers will sometimes strip a meadow bare. Locusts will devour a field to bare dirt. Elephants will obliterate a grove to the point where it takes ten or twenty years for it to recover. On the other hand, I just watched a she-moose browse on a copse of bushes. She would take a few mouthfuls, amble a few steps, eat a bit more, walk a bit more. She never took enough to endanger any one plant. She could have eaten all, filling her belly without moving more than a dozen paces. Why didn't she? Was she conserving her resources? "Of course not!", you may say. "But she is just a dumb animal! It was only instinct!" Okay, maybe you are right. Show me some proof, or even evidence. Not opinion, and not conjecture. No, it is *not*  obvious. Show me a fact. Show me that a moose is not aware, not cognizant of its place in the world, of being a part of a dynamic eco-system. And if you are right, if only Man is spiritual, well, doesn't that make spirituality un-natural?

Uh-oh! I don't think you want to go there.

Man is a part of Nature, as inseparable as the ocean is from water. Thus everything that Man does, from eating to building a city to writing a book to flying to the moon, must be natural. Laboratory-made ascorbic acid is as natural as the Vitamin C in an orange. Not identical, in that the wild orange contains excipients, but the ascorbic acid itself is identical, and just as natural.

Do not try to separate Man from Nature. Do not try to distinguish human acts and their consequences from those that arise from non-human sources. Nothing that Man does is, at heart, truly unique.

It's only natural.

Keeping Things Separate

There are three parts to our land: The Cities, the Farms and the Wilds. They have no borders, but rather blend into each other; there are no places where you can draw a line and say "This side is City, and that side is Wild".

The City is civilization. Here I am using the word in its original sense, "in cities", and nothing more. It does not mean wiser or smarter or more able. It does not mean better or more advanced or wealthier. It also does not mean criminal or foolish or incapable or degraded or worse. It only means "in cities". Cities are where Man has conquered, and bent the world to his will. It is a place devoted entirely to Man, to his needs, desires, whims; there are a few insurrectionists such as rats and pigeons, bedbugs and diseases, parasites on the human race. Most cities have tiny enclaves called parks or greens or commons, and lawns, and trees along streets, but these, too, are there only for the benefit and pleasure of Man. The city has no other purpose than the benefit of Man. This is a good thing. The city provides a place where we can keep a great many people, and do our man-things there without destroying or encroaching on the rest of Life. The more people per square mile, the more efficient the city is.

The rural areas are very different. These are lands that are controlled and planned and dominated by Man, but dedicated to the needs of other life. These other life-forms are largely food for Man, and materials for Man's use, but they must be balanced eco-systems in order to survive, and that requires a great deal of other life-forms: Insects, worms, birds, and so on.

The rural is, like all of Nature, a co-operative and a battle-ground, where Man raises his crops and fights the weeds, and rodents, bugs and birds move in to get their shares. Here is a balance. The rural land is tamed, but tamed like a cat; it will provide what Man wants (usually), but will still do as it pleases, "and there's no doing anything about it". The city, if cut off from everything else, would quickly die; the rural lands, put on their own, would change greatly, but would survive just as well as before.

The Wild, too, is different. In its pure form it is untouched by man. There are a few people in it, a very few, but they fit. They give as much as they take, and are a part of the Wild, just like the bear and the deer and the hawk. Man does not harvest trees or regulate the deer and wolf populations. The only dams are accidental, or built by beavers. Gold and copper and iron are not natural resources, they are just rocks. Over-population is prevented by wolves and pumas eating the excess deer, or by lacking enough prey to support all of the predators. It balances itself. Erosion is prevented by grasses. Devastating forest fires are curtailed by small wildfires reducing the fuel load before it becomes enough to support a large fire. The whole Wild is an intricate machine with a complex set of checks and balances developed over billions of years to keep itself not unchanging, but there, working, persisting. It is far more sophisticated than anything Man has ever conceived, much less created.

Man has made great inroads into the Wild, and caused massive destruction and disruption. But perhaps his greatest asset is that he can learn. He has recognized the destruction, and is adopting non-destructive alternatives. He is finding ways to heal and restore. Yes, there are many campgrounds and ATV trails, but they are being controlled and limited. Most of the Wilds are not in their pure form We harvest many wild trees, but not enough to endanger the Forest. We hunt the wild game, enough to prevent over-population, but take care to not take too many. We modify areas for skiing and hiking and camping, but refrain from making them too big or too common, and regulate those who use them to minimize damage. We learn to live *with* them, to be, as much as is feasible, a part of them, not an intruder.

Huge areas have been set aside as Wilderness, with strictly limited access, if any, and that restricted to foot or sometimes horseback only. We recognize these three parts, and their purposes and uses. We know that they are separate. Now we need to recognize that they *need* to be separate. Now we just need to *keep* them separate.

Accomodation and Preservation

I once wrote "Keeping Things Separate", about separation of City, Country and Wilds. The same principles hold on smaller scales. In cities, there is zoning: Specified areas for business, residential, warehousing and entertainment, and business zones broken down into banks, office, retail and so on. Out in the country, the land is divided into dwelling, cropland, pastures and woodlots. In the Wilds, we have our wilderness, forest, grasslands, and state and national parks. And within the forests we have campgrounds, recreation areas, off-road trails and dispersed camping.

As population and economy change, the needs for these functions change along with them. More people and a more affluent economy mean more vacationers and more facilities. When cities need more facilities and more space for them, they expand. But we cannot expand the Wilds, so we must manage them with more care to accomplish both accomodation of the visitors and preservation of what they come to visit. I will illustrate this using a small portion of the Big Horn National Forest as an example. In this sample space, about eight miles square, there are seven campgrounds. One is strictly a group campground. Aside from Owen Creek, all are handicap-accessible and offer fishing. All but two have twenty to thirty campsites. Most provide hookups for water and electricity. There is also a central dump station for disposal of RV sewage.

Now, do not get the impression that this small area is typical of the whole forest. There are areas of hundreds of square miles with no campgrounds or ORV trails at all. There is a huge wilderness area ten miles south of my sample area, where only a certain small number of people are allowed to be present at one time, and then only on foot. But that is part of the picture: The campgrounds are fairly well grouped, which helps concentrate the human traffic and the risk of fool-started wildfires. The folks who come out here to see the forest and get away from the city in their motor homes and other mobile apartments (they call it "camping" and "roughing it") want water and electrical hook-ups. They are also the majority of visitors. Over half of the rigs I see are rented. For them, we have large campgrounds, often crowded, often with few or no trees. This is good. They will spend most of their time away from the camp, "seeing sights" and "doing things". They have a limited time and feel a need to "get their money's worth". They are accustomed to crowding, so fifteen or twenty feet between sites is not uncomfortable to them. There are others who take little trailers or no trailer at all. They do not need electricity, only a toilet and a water source. There are fewer of them, so a less crowded campground is practical, and that means more room for trees. Then there are the still lighter rigs, a four-wheel drive jeep or pickup truck or a motorcycle. They spend more time in camp, especially those like myself who essentially live out here, migrating with the seasons and rarely spending even a week at one spot; I often spend the whole day in camp, reading, writing, maintaining gear, or doing nothing. We are closer to the wild, we get up at first light and enjoy the waking world. For us, the ideal is a more remote and less developed campground, a hundred feet or more between sites, and lots of trees. And, best of all, there are the hikers. For them, we have walk-in campgrounds, with no access at all for a car or truck or even an ATV, and dispersed camping, nothing more than picking a spot in the forest, with no facilities other than the naturally-occuring ones. The walk-in campground has fire rings, and often an out-house. Some have water, usually a hand-pump well.

All of these types of campgrounds are separate, suited to and sorted by the needs of the users. We need to keep them so, and even consciously enhance the separation. Campgrounds with one or two hundred sites in each, with all amenities, not too crowded, very much like trailer parks. After all, that is, basically, what they are: RV parks. Then another class for those with small trailers, pop-ups and A-frames and such, who only sleep in the trailers, not live in them. Another type that is vehicle-accessible but "tents only", and last, walk-in only. The campgrounds of each of these classes is smaller than the prior class, with fewer campsites, fewer amenities, and more space between campsites. Also many more trees.

Of course, aside from the extremes of RV parks and walk-in camps, most campgrounds are, and will be, somewhat of a mix. The one I am in at the moment is such a mix. You could possibly fit a small motor home such as a "Mini-Winnie", but no fifth-wheels or large trailers. Really nothing much over thirty feet. There are only eight sites and one is used by the camp hosts. The sites are well-spaced, with forty or fifty trees per site. Water is from a cast-iron hand pump, and it is the best tasting water I have ever had. I am told the hosting company wants to expand it, but the Forest Service will not allow it. Good call! Perhaps make a few more campgrounds like this one, if the demand warrants it, but please do not spoil this one!

The balance required is between accomodation of the people (and as there are more people and more affordable means to get up here, more places for them to stay will be required), and preservation of the Wilds, of the lands and waters, the trees and flowers and wildlife which the visitors have come here to see. Preservation, because they cannot be expanded, except by reducing Country or City area. Already the Forest Service is limiting duration of stay, usually to fourteen days in thirty, or forty-five, or sixty. One forest I know of limits visitors to thirty days per year. I do not like it, but I agree with the limits, because the sole alternative is to lose the Wilds, bit by bit, until they are gone. Eventually, it could happen. We could reduce them to manicured parks such as exist in the cities, or they could become sealed off, with human entry a rare and highly regulated occurence. Either no preservation, or no accomodation. Neither is at all likely, but to maintain a workable balance requires attention, and the attention is needed now. The long-term view must be on the time-scale of the Wilds, looking forward at least a thousand years. Personal and corporate profit should not be considered (allowed, certainly, but only as an incidental, a secondary consideration), for the Wilds are an asset belonging to more than even Mankind; they belong to all Life, and we are only a small part of Life.

Mismanagement

I had never visited Rocky Mountain National Park ("Rocky", as the rangers affectionately call it). It is conveniently located as a stop on the way north, and is reported to have spectacular views, so off I go. At the Visitor Center, they tell me that all of the eastern campgrounds are full (on Sunday afternoon!), but the only western campground, Timber Creek, is only half full. Fair enough. If it lives up to its name, it should be a fine base for a few days of hiking. But it was a big disappointment. It may have been Timber Creek at one time, but now all of the big trees are gone, and all that is left is only about ten years old, or less. And the forest surrounding it is terribly ill. Three quarters of the trees are dead, and forlorn standing snags abound, gray wraiths haunting the hillside. A century of suppressing all fires, especially in National Parks, has left the land ripe for disaster, with trees of all ages crowded and tangled together, limbs intertwined, an express intertree superhighway for devastating fires. Yellowstone suffered that fate some thirty years ago, and has mostly recovered nicely.

Rocky has escaped the flames (so far) but was struck with a worse calamity: An infestation of mountain pine borers. Most of the insects' larvae are killed by the winter cold, but a few years ago the winter was too warm. Too many beetles, with easy access to neighboring trees, was too much; the forest died. The dead timber in the campground was cut away, because campers are prone to protest having limbs and trunks dropping on their cars and tents and pets, and even on their children. Timber Creek is now Stump Creek. But the Rangers cannot clear the snags from the forest; There are far, far too many to cut, much less haul away. Now the forest *needs* a fire. It will clear away the dead wood and wipe out the beetles, preventing further spread of the plague. Yes, it will be ugly for a couple of decades, but no worse than it is now. And once it has burned over, we can *leave it alone*. The forest will come back, and it will be a healthy forest. Periodic small fires will clean out the clutter and keep the population down, and thus will prevent a recurrence.

It was not a warm winter that caused the disaster, it was our meddling because of our ignorance. Our meddling is prolonging the damage, making it worse. We are learning, but too slowly. Let it burn.

I left the next morning. Early. The alpine regions are still beautiful. There is nothing there of commercial value, so we have not meddled. There are strictly restricted trails one can hike, and ATVs and snowmobiles are forbidden. We know how delicate the tundra is. We do not "improve" it or "help" it. We leave it alone.

Down the long, long road, twenty miles of coasting, through a small city (there was no other route available) and north to Wyoming. In the West there is a vast dark cloud. Thunderheads are marching east, but their color is off. There is a tinge of brown. I stop at a forest visitor center and learn that there is a big, *very* big fire. It is leveling a large part of the beetle-infested forest. And what is the Forest Service doing about it? *Nothing!* They are watching the edges to keep it away from towns and ranch-houses, but the rest they let burn. Let it burn, let the forest recover naturally, let future fires monitor the forest on their own. In twenty years there will be a fine forest of aspen or lodgepole pine. In fifty, it will be pine and fir, and in one hundred, there will stand a beautiful, mature, *healthy* forest.

Sometimes, the best thing to do is nothing.

It Is All Up To You

For many, many years, people threw their wastes and trash into the rivers, and thought nothing of it, for the waters were great, and the wastes few, and the waters dissolved and dispersed the wastes to invisibility. If the people could not see it, they did not know it was there, and therefore it was not there. Out of sight, out of mind. In time, the waters became sufficiently contaminated to sicken people, at first from disease, from undetectable germs, later from poisons, finally from sheer stench. By then it was becoming noticeable that the water was something less than pure, and people began to do something about it. Not clean it up, but avoid it. Boil the water to make tea and beer, but not bother to clean up the rivers, or even stop contaminating them. Eventually they learned, after a long time, after *many* long times, for the lesson was learned in many places at many times. They ceased to foul the waters, over the strident objections of those who had wastes to dispose of, and would have to find a more expensive means of doing so. Today, our flowing waters are much cleaner, and growing cleaner still, but there are many brooks and streams which appear pristine, but are yet too fouled for us to drink. Not as many, though, as people are told. I have heard, many times, that there are *no* streams from which it is safe to drink. How absurd! If that was true, then the wild folk, the birds and beasts with which our forests teem, would sicken and die. *They* drink the waters. Why can't we?

Most people, town and city dwellers, have weak and coddled immune systems. All of the water they drink is sterilized, either boiled or chlorinated or filtered. They never imbibe the bacteria, so their bodies have no experience, no exercise, in fighting them off. The birds and the beasts have drunk from these streams all of their lives. They drink the bacteria, and their digestive systems and antibodies eliminate them. Routine. No big deal.

A few people still behave ignorantly. They dump their detergents and wastes in or near the water. "It is just a little bit. It is only this once. It will not hurt anything." The fools have learned nothing in twenty thousand years. We have improved, but still have a long way to go. The oceans themselves are being contaminated, not as much or as fast as the alarmists frantically say, but still too much. If we do not improve our ways still further, eventually we *could* kill the oceans.

One problem is that the contamination increases gradually, so gradually that few notice that it is getting worse. They also forget how bad it was once we manage to do something about it, and slack off on the precautions that cleaned it up. Air pollution in cities is thousands of years old. Today it is largely caused by exhaust fumes from internal combustion engines in cars and trucks. Up to around a hundred years ago, it was emanations from dung, human and animal. When we read of a Victorian gentleman being splashed with mud from the London streets, it was not actually mud. It was a mixture of urine and manure dropped by the hundred thousand horses who pulled hansom cabs and dray trucks, supplemented by human sewage tossed from second-story windows. "Garde loo!", the citizens cried (sometimes). "Look out below!" The British still call the toilet the loo. We no longer have sewage contaminating the city air. Not in America and in other industrialized nations, and the worst of our exhaust fume problems was never as bad as the old disease-ridden air, but very few people are aware of it.

They should be. I have read serious proposals to go back to horse-drawn vehicles for the cities, specifically to eliminate air pollution. Please!

The problems encroach gradually, so gradually that people do not notice. Light pollution is a prime example. It has grown so much in the last hundred years that a person from a century ago would be appalled. The first time dusk fell, he would stare agape at the absence of darkness. But who is even aware of it today? And as people suffered from the diseases borne by the rivers of Babylon and Thebes and Rome, which no one knew came from the river, many people today suffer from diseases and infirmities caused by the lack of darkness, true darkness. And the creatures of the wild suffer even more. How can an owl hunt when the night is always bright? How can he know when it is time to hunt? Creatures that navigate by the light of the moon find themselves mis-navigating by the light of a city or a town. And almost as bad, people cannot see the stars. Did you know there are stars in the sky? More than a dozen? That there are potentially well over three thousand of them, not counting the Milky Way, that you can see with the naked eye? Did you know that the stars come in colors, not just white? George Washington did. He could see them. We cannot (except in a few still-dark places), but the change has come about so gradually that few people have noticed.

Pollution is the act of making a thing unfit for the use for which it is intended. We do it all of the time. We cannot help it. Animals do it too. It is okay, it is not dangerous, as long as it is not done too much, and there is some mechanism, some process in place to clean it up at least as fast as it is produced. That is all. Very simple. What *you* need to do is be aware of the pollution you create, and curb it so you do not produce too much. Never mind the big pollutors, factories and power plants and agribusinesses! They are big, and attract attention, and get corrected. The most important polluter that must be monitored is *you*, the individual, and the correct official to monitor you is also you. All three hundred fifty million of you in the United States. Pay attention to what you do. Notice what waste you produce. Look at how much trash you take out every day, how much food you throw out, how much litter you spread, how many plastic bottles and glass jars and metal cans you use once, then throw away, every day. Then multiply that by three hundred fifty million.

Astounding, isn't it? Pretty horrifying, too. Conservation is not just preserving some wild lands that most people will never see, or even hear of. Conservation is *conserving*, not wasting, not using too much of, especially in your normal, mundane, day-to-day life. The pollution produced by big companies and corporations is relatively trivial. The major source is *you!* It is your responsibility, bucko, like it or not. Unless you, the vast majority of you, clean up your act, it will not get handled.

So get cracking, okay?

The Duffer

He was not the sharpest bulb in the six-pack. In his early twenties, he wore black sneakers, jeans and sleeveless T-shirt, no helmet. At least he wore gloves. He rode a mid-size street bike. It was burdened with three large duffel bags, one over the front wheel, two on top of the saddlebags, and a sleeping bag, a chair and a tent, bundled behind the sissybar. Everything was tied on with ropes. He came cruising through the campground, checking out the open sites. Now, being a biker myself, I always pay attention when another camping biker shows up. Consequently, I was watching him, and saw everything, in detail. He rolled along the road, hard dirt with gravel on top, looked at the site on the right, looked at the site on the left, looked right, saw my bike and tent, and hit the brake. The front brake. With the wheel turned. Of course, the wheel shot out and the bike went down. He had no highway bars, so the loaded bike pinned his leg. His denim pants were between his leg and the exhaust pipe, so he was not burning yet, but there was little time to spare. I went over and tried to lift the bike; it would not move. The knots on the forward bag were hidden underneath, not accessible, so I drew my belt knife and slashed the rope. The bag rolled off, and the bike lifted enough for him to pull his leg out. Badly bruised, but not broken, not burned, not bleeding. He was lucky. As he dragged himself aside, I loosed the rest of his load as a neighbor arrived, and together we righted the bike so it would spill no more gas. (Bikes do that when lying on their sides.) We set up his chair and got him a jug of water. He had only a small bottle, and almost empty.

The next site by mine was vacant, so I told him he was taking that one for a few days.   "But I'm only staying overnight!" "Nope, you're staying till that leg is better. At least till Monday." "But there is a better site back a ways!" "True, but I'm not carrying your gear farther that this site, and you are not carrying it at all. Besides, you have a lot to learn before you can get back on the road."

About this time, the campground host showed up, assured himself that Duffy was not badly injured, and took care of the camping fee. We wheeled the bike and gear over, then I came back to start the kid's education.

He had a few years experience on a bike, and had been camping every year through his teens, but this was his first season-long trip. When told he had too much gear, and that it was loaded badly, especially the bag over the front tire, he adamantly maintained he was not overloaded; a friend had showed him a photograph of a biker loaded very much like he was, even to the bag in front of the windshield. Yes, that was probably me; literally hundreds of people have snapped pics of me and of my bike, usually when it was loaded. Appearance and actuality, though, are often very different; I told him so, and proceeded to enumerate his errors.

"The big, bulky bag in front of my windshield is two sleeping bags rolled up in a tarp. It weighs only six pounds, maybe seven. Your bag is a good sixty pounds. It increases the inertia, so when you hit a bump, you stand a good chance of having the front wheel bounce right off the ground; certainly it reduces traction on the up side of the bounce; and that makes it more likely you will low-side, like you just did on the gravel. Your saddlebags are stuffed with lightweight gear; the two duffels on top are much heavier, about equally so. Distributing the weight equally between the bags makes them easier to carry, but is wrong for stowing on a bike. Put the heaviest stuff in the saddlebags, and the heaviest of what is left in the lower duffel. The top duffel should be as light as you can make it. Has your bike ever toppled over when not moving, because you leaned it just a little too far? Well, that is why; the center of gravity was too high."

There were many more errors. We talked over each one, why it was an error, what could happen because of it, and how to do it right. When he finally admitted he had a lot to learn, I handed him a copy of my motorcycle camping book, and left him to sit in the shade and study.

Monday morning his leg was healed enough for him to ride safely and comfortably, if he did not go too far. His gear had been redistributed properly, and about eighty pounds worth given away or abandoned. It was all nice-to-have stuff, not truly important or valuable, as evinced by the fact that not a single bit was of any use to me. He rode off, wearing his bike jacket, into the sunrise. Two weeks later he sent me an email, expressing how much easier and more comfortable it was to ride with the lighter load, and properly packed.

It is the same with every technology, camping, cooking, carpentry, whatever. The expert makes it look easy, but when you try it for the first time, nothing seems to work. The very first thing you have to learn is the basics, the fundamentals. For carpentry, learn to drive a nail straight, and learn to saw a straight and square line. For painting, learn to sketch and draw before ever looking at paint, or even colored pencils. If you learn the basic techniques, and the vocabulary, you can learn *anything*, even the most advanced calculus, even camping. If you do not, you will never be any good at it. It may even kill you. It almost killed Duffy.

Spirit

Meta Physics

The physicists have made a mistake: They have omitted a basic element of the universe. They hold that the universe comprises Space, Time, Energy and Matter, with a quibble that Energy and Matter are actually two forms of the same thing. What would physics be if one of these, perhaps Time, was unknown? How then could one explain water changing to ice, or an object moving? Scientists would be forced to deny that any kind of change had ever occured, because change requires time. With sufficient cleverness and imagination, one could devise a science, call it Sub-Physics, that was internally consistent and fairly well explained the world. Perhaps the scientists would maintain the "past" and "Future" are only illusions or concepts, that the world as it is *now* is all there is. We "remember" past, but nothing ever changes. It takes a bit of stubbornness, but could be believed. Most of physics would work, and many explanations would be accurate. The characteristics of iron would be accurately known. Magnetism would be fairly well described. Of course, it would require some very complex, intricate and far-fetched theories to explain the inevitable inconsistencies. All because of the lack of one basic factor.

Physics today is complex, intricate, and includes many theories which certainly seem very far-fetched. Heisenberg's Uncertainty Principle is a prime example: You cannot know both the location and motion of a subatomic particle; you can know one or the other, but not both. Or Einstein's theory that no matter can exceed the speed of light. Lots of math to go with this, and lots of complications, including a theoretical particle called a tachyon which cannot go *slower* than light. But every truth I have ever seen has been simple, very simple. Every complex "truth" has turned out to contain an error or falsehood, and when that error was discovered, the resulting truth was simple.

Truth is always simple. Complexity, always, *always*, contains untruth. Even when the complexity is only a large number of simple truths viewed as one thing, there is a lie: That it is only one thing, not a collection of smaller things.

One form of untruth is a statement that a false thing is true. Another form, harder to spot, is an omission; some fact has been left out, such as "He died from drinking coffee", not mentioning that there was cyanide in the coffee.

What if the physicists have left out a basic element of the Universe? What if the Universe comprises Space, Time, Matter and Energy . . . and something else? A lot of physics would work, experiments would give consistent results, if you ignored the inconsistent . . . excuse me, "anomalous" . . . results. But if you do not ignore anomalies, you have to discover (make up, invent) an explanation, usually fetched from far beyond observed data. These explanations are generally rather intricate, and if they sound simple, are based on intricate theories and complex mathematics.

But truth is always simple. Therefore there is a simple explanation: There is a fifth basic element.

We are entering a new field, beyond current physics, and bearing much the same relation to physics as chemistry bears to alchemy. Alchemy was useful and did produce some results, but fell far short of accomplishing what can be accomplished with chemistry. Physics is likewise far short of this new field. "Meta" means "above" or "beyond"; we could call Chemistry "Meta-Alchemy". This new field, beyond current physics, is called "Meta-Physics". It is often considered to be abstract theory with no basis in reality, but that is the scoff made by those who insist that only the purely physical, that is, space, time, matter and energy, exist. Merriam-Webster gives a different definition: " a division of philosophy that is concerned with the fundamental nature of reality and being". That is to say, it deals with the physical *and* the non-physical. This is very appropriate, because the missing fifth element is Spirit. As a lake is made of water, so is a Soul made of Spirit. You may substitute whatever term you prefer for "soul". I am referring to the person, the being itself, apart from the body. The "I", the awareness, the thing that exists and knows that it exists. "Me." "I Am."

This is the thing that decides to have a hot dog instead of a hamburger, and thus, according to the Chaos theorists, changes the course of history (and they are right). This is the thing that creates, that has ideas (which are Spirit, not Space, Time, Energy or Matter). This is the thing that looks at Thunder Ridge and turns it into Crazy Horse Monument. There is no way Space, Time, Energy and Matter could do that. Some scientists maintain that we cannot detect or measure spirit, and therefor it does not exist. Perhaps we have no such instrument *yet*; perhaps we do, but have misinterpreted the data. But failure to detect is not proof, else we would have to maintain that the moons of Jupiter did not exist before Galileo made his telescope and detected them.

Most physicists will scoff at this "pseudo-religious nonsense". But a few, maybe one in ten thousand, the *real* scientists, will wonder, experiment, and, who knows?, maybe take the biggest step forward since Newton.

You can help, too. Show this essay to a physicist. OK?

Love

It is a puzzler. Maybe it is easier in other languages, but in English, people love God, Country, a spouse, children, music, mountains, sex, pizza, and so on. Well, they *say* they do. There are at least six different definitions in those examples alone. Six different things. *Very* different, and you mix them up at your own dire risk. Tell your wife you love her the way you love pizza, and you will be sleeping on the couch.

I think I have finally figured it out. It is not sex; it has nothing to do with sex, nothing at all. Do you love your children? Of course! Do you have sex with them? Do you even *want* to have sex with them? Of course not! Sexual desire is lust, not love. Love is not a strong liking, such as the love of music or fine food. And it is not, as is commonly held, even an emotion.

Love is an attitude. It is the importance, the value, that we assign to the welfare, the survival, of a thing, be it person or concept or animal or countryside, even one's own self. It is a scale, with positive and negative values, which I arbitrarily assign negative one hundred to positive one hundred. On the negative side is what we call *Hate*; on the positive side is what we call *Love*. The more highly you value the welfare of a thing, the more you love that thing; the more you desire the destruction of a thing, the more you hate that thing.

Self-sacrifice occurs when love of a thing exceeds love of self. A parent dying or risking death to save a child does so out of love. A soldier who throws himself on a live hand grenade to shelter his buddies does so out of love. A person spending time and money to protect a marshland does so out of love; how much he will spend depends on how great his love is. And hate follows the same rule. John Wilkes Booth assassinated Abraham Lincoln, not to save his beloved South, but because he desired to end the existence of the man on whom he placed the blame for the loss. He knew full well he would probably not get away with it, but felt the action was worth the cost. Had he performed the assassination some years earlier, it might have been from love of his country, but the South had already lost, He killed from hate.

We can also understand how love can turn to hate. It is not such a great transformation, but merely a reversal of attitude. "Hell hath no fury like a woman scorned." She has given her love, placed another's welfare above her own, and been coldly rejected. Rather than admit she had misjudged him, she rejects his welfare, and either cares nothing about it, or else actively seeks his destruction. It is simple, obvious, and normal. Also easily prevented.

I am very pleased with this insight. It has already made a significant difference in my life, especially in my attitude. I feel much more in control of myself and my future. I hope it proves useful to you. I sincerely do.

Because I love you.

Plans and Dreams

I make many plans, plans to go and visit here, there or yonder, plans to see and do this, that, or the other. Most of the plans I never actually carry out, but that is okay, because I have a very active, robust well-exercised and well-trained imagination, and therefor just making the plan is almost as good, as satisfying, as fun, as the actual doing. But not this one. This plan was wonderful and rewarding in itself, but even my imagination could not elevate it to the quality of the fufilled dream. It was a long-term plan, laid down more than a year in advance, and committed to seven months later, when, for the first time ever, I reserved a campsite. The Perfect Campsite. The perfect time. The peak of my annual expedition.

I was going back to Owen Creek.

I wrote of this campsite in the essay "Perfection".   I described the active creek at its very edge, with the deep hole for chilling drinks, and the quirky cliffs, with rounded rocks protruding among the climbing trees, the forest with abundant firewood, the bold, even brazen wildlife. And now it was mine, my private property, my domain and demesne, for the last two weeks in August. And just to add the final polish, in the middle of that period was a total solar eclipse.

I placed the reservation six months in advance, on the very first day that reservations were allowed. Three weeks later, the site was booked solid for the entire season. The other four reservable sites between them did not have as many booked days. Yes, I was lucky, very lucky. But, please note, luck, good or bad, does not just happen. It is made, one way or another, by planning or procrastination, by the person himself.

I had planned to head north from New Mexico, stopping overnight in the Medicine Bow National Forest, then moving on to Bear's Tepee (which most people call Devil's Tower; a bad name for such a holy place), where I would spend a day or two before crossing Wyoming to reach the Bighorn Mountains.

But I stopped at a campground where I had never before been, and was captured by the irresistable beauty of the place. One of the truly glorious aspects of the wandering lifestyle is that there are so many wondrous locales scattered, hidden, unknown, among the Rocky Mountains, that we never know when a new discovery will occur, only that they *will* occur, and the more you travel, the more you will find. But this one is another story (several, in fact), and I will only say here that it pre-empted my Bear's Tepee time, and it was only by the stronger enchantment (and pre-paid reservation) of Owen Creek that I managed to escape.

The passage began late, as they so often do, for friends, the curious, the interested, always come to visit, to say goodbye. They are fascinated by motorcycle camping, by how I can load a bike, and especially by a canvas wall-tent. They talk, they chat, they delay, so it was ten o'clock before I hit the road.

First was a quick run to Laramie, a town I know well, to feed the bike. On long traverses, I estimate mileage and plan stops for gas accordingly, but, as I believe I have mentioned earlier, plans change. I could not quite reach Casper, not with confidence, on one tank, so I planned to fill up halfway at Medicine Bow. However, I had a good tailwind, and went straight through with fuel to spare. It was a wonderful ride, very nearly a perfect ride, a good road, beautiful scenery, almost no other vehicles in sight all of the way. One hundred forty miles of bliss. But then came the leg to Buffalo. Only one hundred fourteen miles, but on an interstate freeway with a speed limit of eighty, and strong, gusty crosswinds and headwinds. Higher speeds reduce mileage, as do crosswinds and especially headwinds. I had to switch to reserve gas with thirty-four miles to go. Reserve would never last that long, so I pulled onto a rest area for a rest and a smoke, and added my gallon of emergency gas to the tank. That sufficed to get me to Buffalo, but there I encountered a strange thing.

I have written before about places that were familiar, that I knew and recognized, though it was the first time I had seen them. They were sections of land, forest, valley, mountain, miles or tens of miles of territory, which could have been picked up and transported to another area, another state, hundreds of miles away, and would belong there, would fit in with no way to tell where the foreign and native lands met. But this time I found it in a town. I had visited Buffalo before, almost. A freeway passed only two miles north of it, and I had passed that way several times. But this time I entered from the South. I pulled off of the freeway at a sign that promised gas, and rode a mile and a half through familiar territory. I had ridden this road before. The green wild meadows, the long dip to the bridge over the stream, the long rise to the right, to scattered houses, small offices, commercial buildings, the edge of a small town, then the gas station on the right, with heavy gravel making the turn in hazardous. The land was familiar, the buildings familiar, the *details* familiar. I had been there before, where I now came for the first time. And I found it in memory: A little mountain town in New Mexico. If you were to swap the two roads, or take pictures and show them to the locals, they would recognize the photographs, they would accept the roads. Their only doubts would be on the order of "Gee, I never noticed that rock before".

When I left Buffalo, it was as if the stretch from Casper had never existed. The tailwind was back, and it lasted forty miles, almost to the last leg of the journey. And that is where the magic began. I left the freeway, and passed through the villages of Ranchester and Dayton. Little things, they are, just a few hundred people, quiet, attractive, even charming. Neat, and not poor. And they serve as a worthy transition from the twenty-first century tamed world of freeways and semi-trailers, banks, supermarkets, oil wells and construction companies, to the dateless wild country, with its own priorities and prerogatives, its own standards and styles. I departed Dayton and faced the towering mass before me, rising almost a full mile, and stretching from horizon to horizon, an entirely different world from that which was dwindling behind me. I had reached the Bighorn Mountains.

As the road began to climb the pine-covered foothills, I inhaled, deeply. The air was redolent with the most intense forest perfume that has ever graced my nostrils. The rich spicy pine aroma was as new as if it was the first odor ever created, and it struck me as the sudden gift of vision would strike a man blind from birth. And I laughed, for the sheer joy of being, and for the knowledge that, as magnificent as it was, this was only the beginning, that there was yet thirty miles of improvement, of intensification, of simply getting better and better.

And so it proved. Four thousand feet. The road was wet in spots from recent rain, which explained the intensity of the aromas. Five thousand feet. The road winding through the endless acres of thick green pines. Six thousand feet. Immense cuttings for the road, great cliffs, scars carved into the hillside, revealing ancient seams and colored layers, rainbows in earth tones. Seven thousand feet. Switchbacks and steep slopes driving upward, ever upward. Eight thousand feet. Vast vistas, viewpoints laying all of Creation before me, an endless panorama of infinite variety. Eighty-eight hundred feet, the ridge, the pass through the great barrier to the high green plateau beyond. Green! Not the usual browns and tans I knew well from previous sojourns. Green! Lush, rich, thick, verdant forests and plains. So it was true. The rains and blizzards and floods of this past winter were truly the breaking of the decades-long drought, the sixty or seventy years of scanty, parsimonious rain. The next twenty or forty year period had begun. Rains were frequent this spring and summer. The lakes are now full, gushing their overflow into swollen streams, the water table rising as the aquifers begin their long recovery. The air is chill with altitude, and great clouds dominate the sky as they brush the mountain peaks. But no rain falls on me, and the roads I traverse are dry beneath my wheels as I make the turn south. Four more miles, just four more, through familiar fields now green and tall, the same as I remember, but so different, the little girl grown to be a woman.

And there it is: A turnoff, a short quarter mile of dirt road, now mud road, wet but firm, and I have arrived at Owen Creek. Like everything else, exactly as I remember, but so different. This time, as never before, there is no one here. No one.

Every site is empty. Even the camp hosts are absent, probably gone to town for groceries. And there is my site, the Perfect Campsite, open, empty, inviting, and a sign on the post proclaiming that it is reserved. For me.

The first thing I do is go to the pump for a jug of the treasured wonderful well water. It is not pure. Oh, no, nothing so undesireable as pure! It contains dissolved minerals, which lend it that welcome flavor. Delicious! There is no better water in the world! Next I pitch my tent and stow my gear, for if I do not, it will surely start to rain. I want to see the stars tonight, so anything that might appease the cloud-gods is worth doing. The hosts return, and we joyfully greet each other.

Night falls. I eat dinner beside the chattering creek, beneath the cloudless sky, for the weather has cleared completely, wishing to make my homecoming as sweet as possible. The stars appear, more and more, old friends glowing brightly their greetings to me. The Milky Way forms overhead, washing the sky with a radiance invisible elsewhere, but possible here because of the absence of any competing light. The nearest source of sky glow is Sheridan, but it has fewer than twenty thousand people, and what little light it produces is balked by four thousand feet of elevation, and a nine-thousand foot ridge. Here there is no sky glow at all. None. The only thing inhibiting the stars is the moisture in the air. And thus the seeing is only Class 2, not 1. Only. There may be a dozen or two places in the Lower Forty-Eight where the stars can be seen so well. Not more.

I have arrived. A year of preparation and anticipation has culminated in realization. My friends have greeted me. Nature has greeted me. I am where I want to be, and it simply could not be better.

You see? Plans are nothing. Plans are not important. Plans can be discarded out of hand, for half of their fun, at least, is in the making of them. Dreams are a different matter. Plans are for making, but dreams are for coming true. And they do.

Where Did the Time Go?

My roaming season is almost over, and it is nearly time to make for my winter encampment. I spent an hour reviewing my journey, recalling the good times and the bad times, the old friends I met, the old friends I ran into again, the animals and the trees and the stones, streams and settlements. A lot of them I was revisiting; more I was meeting for the first time. A few planned parts, many extemporaneous extras, even some unavoidable adventure. It was a very good year, and it lasted a very long time. By the calendar, it was only eight months, but the events of March seemed at least two years old.

It is well known that time flies faster and faster as one gets older and older. Remember the days when you were eight years old? Each one lasted at least a month! And then when you became a working stiff, events of the prior month felt as recent as last week. Was it really so long ago? And then, in your retirement, you dwell on days gone by, you fondly recall the good old days, you reminisce with friends of the dreams you had and the adventures of your youth, and when December rolls by, it seems last Christmas was only yesterday. Where did the time go?

It is not, as I have heard it theorized (and once believed), because days become smaller parts of your total time. A five-year-old has lived fewer than two thousand days; at fifty-five, one has lived over twenty thousand. Does it not make sense that each day would seem only a tenth as long?   Well, maybe, but that is not how it works.

To the child, each day is a new thing. Each day is packed with wonderful things that have never been seen before, never been done. Everything is new, and must be dwelt upon and studied and experienced to the limit of one's ability. To the adult, though, each day is a repeat. The working person, and especially the office worker, has only three days in a week: Saturday, Sunday, and Weekday. Monday through Friday, he does the same thing, every day. Details vary, but only details. When did I do that report? Was it Monday? Wednesday? Last week? For him, the year is less than half as long as it is to the child. Much less, because this week was the same as last week which was the same as each week last month and the months before. Aside from the occasional unique occurence like the time that Piper Cub crashed in the parking lot, three quarters of the days last year were essentially identical. And the poor folks in the retirement home spend almost all of their time in the past, reliving moments of pleasure. A day spent in the past is *in* the past, far in the past; it is not in the current year. That is where the time went.

There is a remedy. There is a way to get back to the fullness of time which every child enjoys. It is a matter of experience, or rather, *experiences*. If you have a daily routine, a set of things you do every day, always at the same time, day after day, time will fly. After all, each day is the same, so you really have only that one same day. But if you vary your activity, plant a tree and some flowers one day, go to the beach the next, then go sailing, go camping for a week, visit a museum or two, whatever, as long as you are doing and creating a new experience each day, the days will not blend and blur into each other. Maybe do some long activity for a week or two, like build a trailer or make a tent or a coat. The important point is that it is a new thing, something you have not done before, or that you do very infrequently. Sure, you can meet with your friends and chat for an hour or three each evening, every day. Yes, you can get up to watch the sunrise every day. I do not mean to imply you never repeat, just do not repeat *everything*, or even the majority of what you do. If each day is unique, is different from other days, then you are like the child: Each day is new, each day is packed with wonderful things to be experienced as fully as you can.

Last month I was in mountains over nine thousand feet above sea level, and fully prepared to experience snow. Last week I was in a lush river valley where it rained every two or three days Just a little, but the weather changed every day. Today I sit on an arid desert plain which is lucky to get three inches of rain in a year. It is *different*. Sometimes several days in a row are similar, the same weather and pretty much same activities, but every week, at the least, is distinct from every other one. And, as I said, last March seems two years ago.

On a larger scale, I spend Winters in Arizona low deserts, Springs in New Mexico State Parks, and the rest of the year all over the Rocky Mountains. But in Winter I do long projects such as building a trailer or a tent, so each Winter is distinct. And there are thirty State Parks in New Mexico that I can camp in, all different, some dramatically so, and I only visit a half dozen each year. Again, there is little duplication. Each sojourn is different. And as for the Rockies, why, I could spend five hundred years wandering them and still not have seen everything. The variety is infinite, in the trees, in the flowers, in the mammals and the birds, the streams and rivers and lakes and marshes, even in the mountains and the very rocks. The only thing that stays the same is the stars and the moon.

Vary your life, make each day an individual, and time will not fly. It will soar.

Physical and Spiritual

I have always been a voracious reader. Histories have always fascinated me, especially when I could find books written by different cultures. The history of the Crusades as seen from the Saracen viewpoint is fascinating, and not at all complimentary of the Crusaders. Religion has also been an area of intense interest. How is it so many different people can believe such contradictory (and sometimes obviously false) concepts, and still, almost every one, maintain that *their* version is the Truth, and *everyone* else is wrong? What colossal arrogance! I have also dwelt in many countries, in cities, towns, rural areas, and the Wilds. I have known many, many people, both human and otherwise, and found they are each and every one very similar: They just want to be left alone to live their lives as they see fit. I have learned to observe, and to think (and such a rare activity that is!) I have been certain of many things, and later found I was wrong in quite a few of them. I have learned, as few others apparantly have, that in anything, in everything, I may be mistaken. But from all I have seen and read, certain points have become apparant. They answer many fundamental questions, and are very probably true.

We exist in two universes, the Physical and the Spiritual. The being itself (that's you) is a spirit (or soul or whatever other label you feel comfortable with), and the body is an animal, a machine made of flesh. While you are not the body, it is very important to you. It is your identification card, how others recognize you (usually). It is the primary tool with which you manipulate the physical environment. It is the interface between you and the physical universe that you use to receive sensations and, basically, play the game of Life. But it is not you, any more than your car is you. And this is of vital importance.

The two universes are very different. We have Good ("tending toward construction, happiness, or survival") and Evil ("tending toward destruction, misery, or death"). We have Right (Good) and Wrong (Evil), Justice, Fairness, Beauty, Esthetics. But these only exist in the Spiritual Universe; they are considerations of spirits. The Physical Universe does have Correct and Incorrect, which are alternate definitions of Right and Wrong, but with no spiritual value. "Water tends to flow downhill" is correct, but there is no Good or Evil or Fairness to it. It just is. Water erodes rock. To us this is Good, in that it creates soil for plants to grow in, and Evil in that it washes out roads. To *us* it is Good or Evil. To the world, it just is. There is no Beauty or Esthetic, except to us. Some find the smell of coffee or a banana appetizing; others find them nauseating. Some delight in the aroma of a cigar. Others are sickened by the stench. That is *us*, that is Spiritual (having to do with the spirit). In the world, all scents are simply fine particles given off by various substances, molecules drifting through the air. Not good or evil or beautiful or ugly. Just there.

"The world is not fair." Ah, how many times have we heard that! But what does it mean? Some people mean it to say "It is okay to be not fair", or "There is no point in being fair", or even "It is foolish to try to be fair". All it truly means is that the world does not care, it only is, it does what it does because it is a machine, and that is the way it runs. Fairness is a spiritual concept, and can only exist in the Spiritual Universe.

Man, and possibly every lifeform, consists of two parts, the animal and the spirit. The animal part is of the Physical

Universe and, left to itself, will *act* as part of the Physical Universe. The world is barbaric; there is no Right or Wrong, only Survival. Strength prevails. Might is right. The only crime is getting caught. If you can possibly take advantage of something else, you should do so. Civilization, fairness, justice, Good and Evil, all are purely spiritual aspects, and must be imposed upon the animal, for the animal knows nothing of these, and they often run contrary to Natural Law. Squirrels see nothing wrong with gathering and hiding every bit of food they can find. They hoard enough food to get them through the Winter, then keep gathering and hoarding, even though that means some other creature may not be able to gather enough. They are so single-minded about the task that they forget where much of it is cached, and never use it. Squirrels are utterly baffled by the concept of "enough". Some people behave in the same way, accumulating wealth which they do not need and will never use, even wasting much of it, just to show that they can afford it. Some of them strive so hard for more and more and more that it kills them. At the same time, other people are barely surviving, or worse, because these hoarded resources are not available to them. This is barbarism, unthinking animal greed, which is always with us, and must always be controlled.

Now there is nothing wrong with the clever and able and strong accumulating wealth and power, and accumulating more than most other people. They have the ability, and they are rewarded for it by surviving better, more easily and more comfortably. This is Good, it is Fair and Just. What is wrong, what is Evil, is accumulating more than they can reasonably use, wasting and destroying what they do not need, at the unnecessary expense of others. There are conditions where the weaker or less able must suffer. If there are ten people, but only enough food for nine, one will go hungry. But when there is enough for all ten, and one takes twice what he needs, this causes unnecessary hunger, and is wrong, Evil. Even worse is when the one takes enough for four, but it happens.

This is the way the world works. The barbaric animalish-people greedily squirrel away as much as they can, thinking only of themselves and their family, possibly their tribe or nation, and have no care at all for the welfare of anyone else. Then spiritual-people gain influence or control and engender a civilization, providing for all, or at least more, of the people. Life becomes easier, safer, more comfortable, more secure. Production rises, and the standard of living and population rise with it. Arts and sciences flourish, people have more fun, have to labor less for even better conditions. Some, the more able, the wiser, the more productive, have more than others. Some, the less intelligent, the less competent, have less, may even be struggling just to get by, but they are far fewer than in the barbaric culture, and usually better off. Sometimes, even the worst off are sheltered and clothed and have enough to eat. Compare the standard of poverty in America today with the standard of, say, Bangladesh in 1980. Or with the United States during the Great Depression. But the barbarians are always among us and, over time, will regain the upper hand. Compare the standards of living in North and South Korea. Inevitably, aristocracies will become tyrannies, democracies will become anarchies (anarchies under the definition of "no rules", not the true definition of "no rulers"). The unscrupulous take every advantage they can and accumulate more and more resources and wealth. The rich get richer and the poor get poorer, and when the gulf between gets too wide, the poor rebel. In aristocracies, it is usually violent revolution, and the rebels either lose and get slaughtered or win and slaughter the rich. In democracies, it is usually voter rebellion; wealth is confiscated from the rich and given to the poor till there is nothing left to distribute, and the system collapses, in anarchy or violent revolution or foreign conquest. And we are back to the barbaric animal-people greedily squirreling away as much as they can.

Seems hopeless, doesn't it? Fortunately, we seem to be learning, albeit very slowly. Each civilization learns something from the last, and rises a bit higher, on average. I do not see that the solution is a "perfect" political or social system; these are only tools, and tools do nothing of themselves. Ancient Athens, one of the highest civilizations we know of, seems to have flourished (and fallen) in direct relation to the spirituality of the people. The Incas and Aztecs, who may have risen even higher than Athens or Egypt, seem to have done the same, but we will likely never know, for the barbarians (the Spaniards) destroyed almost all of their records. Given that Good, Evil, Fairness and so on are spiritual factors, I will maintain that any solution must lie in the spiritual development of the people, each and every one of them. If we had no animal-people, we would almost certainly develop a high and long-lasting civilization, and it would persist so long as the people remained spiritual. I do not mean that the people would all have the same, or even similar, religions, for any truly spiritual religion will be tolerant of other religions. I mean that everyone would be spiritual, would recognize, understand, and value these spiritual attributes. It is only through the acts of the foolish, the greedy, the unscrupulous, that civilizations are made to fall.

Self: Ish and Less

Some people have called me self-centered. Actually, they have *accused* me; they say it like it is a bad thing. I understand them. I know why they feel thus. They were taught. When they were little children, they had it drummed into their dear little ears, before they were six, or seven, or eight. And the lecture has continued, in subtle, sneaky ways, to this very day.

Share, even if you cannot afford it. Be considerate of others, even when it damages you. Think of the other person's feelings, never of yourself. It is all around you, if you look for it, if you are willing to notice it. In jokes and movies and TV tales, the selfish and greedy are portrayed as frowning, evil, unappetizing characters who always get there come-uppance in the end. The selfless, generous, caring people are attractive, smiling, even angelic, and invariably win. History is altered to show only, or mostly, the good side of heroes and the bad side of villains. It is pretty much all black and white.

Well, the real world is not like that. I have never known anyone outside of fiction who was all bad or all good, or all selfish or all selfless. And I have not seen that Bad and Selfish or Good and Selfless had any relation.

Whenever I am going to have campfires, I have to gather firewood. I do so greedily and selfishly. I gather *lots* of wood, more than I need, because I do not like to run out. I gather the best of the wood, the most easily available. I gather it as easily as I can, for I like to get maximal return for minimal effort. When someone leaves a campground, I often go to their site and gather any firewood they abandoned, even half-burned chunks from the fire pit. It is easier than hunting it up in the woods and lugging it back. Greedy. Selfish. Do you do it any differently? "Oh, there is some good stuff, easy to get. But I'll struggle to get that poor stuff, and leave this for someone else."

On the other hand, if someone pulls in late, too late to gather wood, and there is no camp host to buy it from, I will often give them an armload or two. That is considerate. That is selfless. That is friendly. Or is it, really? Often they will reciprocate, replacing the wood the next day, or inviting me to dinner. It is not something you can count on (and I do not), but it does happen. And when I depart, leaving three or four days worth of wood neatly stacked, no one even has a *chance* to pay me back or return the favor. It might be seen as paying it forward, as an exchange for the abandoned wood I already gleaned from other campsites. But it is not, not really. That is not why I leave it. I am actually being selfish, because helping others makes me feel good. Feeling good about yourself is very, very important. What many people seem to miss is that you must have a *reason* to feel good. Being helpful, useful, valuable to others is probably the best such reason.

Selfishness is being considerate of and helpful to one's own self. Selflessness is being considerate of and helpful to others without concern for oneself. Self-less; no "self". But they are not mutually exclusive. They can, and should, be done together. Either one, done by itself, and with no trace of the other, is almost always bad. Evil. Risking one's life to save a drowning person is selfless, but also selfish in that one would expect others to do the same for you. One is almost shamed into taking the risk in order to be worthy of rescue later. Or to repay the debt, if one has been rescued at some earlier time. If I could rescue someone, but did not try, I would feel very bad about it. I expect you would feel the same. Even in making the supreme sacrifice, there is still that element of selfishness.

"Self-centered" is actually something quite different. It refers to the viewpoint, literally the point from which one views. Between the ears and just behind the eyes is the usual point for most people. What most people consider to be the center of self. But the term is usually used, more or less metaphorically, as "not considering other viewpoints". Or, as one might say, only considering "self" as being the individual. If one identifies strongly enough with a nation, one will be willing to risk injury or death to preserve that nation. Or a smaller group, or a family. Or a larger group, such as Mankind, or All Life. You can still be selfish while centered on the group, if *you* think of the group as "self". The Nazis centered on Germany in World War Two, the Crusaders centered on Christianity, Al-Quada centered on Islam. None had any concern for the ones they attacked. Selfish.

But there is (at least) one circumstance where purely selfish self-centeredness is not bad, is actually a great goodness. It does no harm, it causes no damage. It does not exact the smallest price or cost on any one or any thing. It takes place in one's own personal universe, in the magical realm we call Imagination. I once wrote of returning to a familiar place, of sharing greetings with many friends, and of the gathering culminating in the grandest and most beautiful sunset I have ever seen. And I assumed the most selfish and self-centered viewpoint possible, and claimed that sunset as my own, as a display, a celebration, which the place created as a means of greeting me, of welcoming me home. Fantasy? Certainly. Imagination? Beyond any doubt. Truth? Well, you will have to decide that for yourself. It is true for me. It made my heart swell, and brought tears to my eyes. It made me feel home, and welcome. It made me very, very happy. It was not, by any values, a bad thing.

Imagine That!

The denizens of the Wilds do not take exercise; they get all they need just staying alive, running after prey or away from predators. They are also quite enthusiastic in their play. Just watch a pair of squirrels playing tag, across the clearings and up and down the trees, honing their skills for escaping coyotes and hawks. They exercise their imaginations, too. A lapine workout consists of a rabbit sitting in a field munching some succulent herbs till there is a sudden sound, or a shadow moves, at which point the heart-rate triples and the muscles tense. Aerobics and Dynamic Tension! Somewhat similar to human gyms, in that it is often followed by a dinner date, but in the bunny's case, it would be the date doing the dining.

In the case of many humans, especially modern Americans, exercise must be sought after and planned. Aside from farmers and construction workers and such, most do not do physical labor. No, typing at a computer does not count. When I lived in a city, I rode a bicycle to work. I almost never saw anyone else do it; they drove cars, even if it was only a half mile. Some, a few, jog or belong to gyms. Some buy an exercise machine, and use it for a month or two, then sell it. I saw a lot of them at yard sales. Many, probably most, did not exercise at all, beyond playing frisbee at the company picnic.

People exercise Imagination even less. There are few jobs that require much. Then they go home and watch television till bedtime. Except for a few shows such as The Twilight Zone, all that is required is to sit still and absorb. Have you ever listened to a radio play? I have often lived where there was no television (this was mostly before satellite dishes). We would listen to radio plays in rapt fascination. There were no pictures, just sound effects and words. You had to make your own pictures in your mind. Imagination! The plays were far better than almost any television shows. And there are books. Real books, just words, no pictures save perhaps an illustration every forty or fifty pages. Comic books, "graphic novels", do not really count. They provide the pictures and even the sound effects, pre-empting the use of your own visions and ideas. I suppose they are okay, but wash your hands after reading one.

Books are arguably the most valuable innovation, the most useful tool, that has ever been created. Non-fiction lets us remember and pass on ideas, experience and knowledge to others far away in space and time. Worse than Hitler, Stalin, Mao-Tse-Tung, even Rachel Carson, was the Caliph who ordered the burning of the Library of Alexandria. The arrogant son of a black dog said "If it is in the Koran, we do not need it. If it is not, it is of no value". Fiction is, or can be, at least as valuable as non-fiction, for it lets us share ideas, viewpoints, imaginings that might be created only once in a hundred lifetimes. But most importantly, fiction exercises imagination and teaches one how to use it, what can be done. Everything, not just muscles, must be exercised; immune systems, to fight off disease, skin, to tolerate temperature extremes, mental abilities, such as arithmetic and rhetoric, memory and logic, to perceive lies, exaggerations and errors from salesmen, marketers and politicians, and especially imagination. New ideas are necessary to create solutions to problems, to improve existing techniques and technologies, to create new things and new activities. New ideas are the germ of all progress. And new ideas, every single new idea that ever was, came from imagination. Without imagination, all of us, what few there would be, would still be sitting in front of our caves, howling at the Moon. Assuming we had managed to progress that far. Imagination is what let us have men walking on the Moon instead of howling at it.

Imagination should be taught in school, from first grade right up to twelfth. All children have an imagination, just as they have muscles, but it must be used, exercised. Not encouraging and exercising imagination, and providing activities and entertainments that not only do not demand, but actively discourage, thinking, are the reason so few adults have or use their imaginations. The children would not be graded on "good" or "bad' ideas, but on originality, completeness, consistency. Start with exercises such as "Invent a new dessert, in detail", and work up to things like "Invent a useful new word" or "Come up with a new idea that no one else ever had before". "Find something that needs to be improved, and figure out how to do it."

We could breed a whole generation of people who used their imaginations all day to understand and improve every aspect of life.

Imagine that!

Preferences

I was chatting with an old friend. He was complaining about generators, how people would come to the Wilds to get away from the city, but when they got here, fired up generators. Not only did they bring their city apartments and their city satellite dishes, but they also brought their city background noise. My friend preferred the natural quiet of the woods. But he had to raise his voice to tell me, and I had to listen carefully to understand him, because we were sitting just a few feet from a steep and loud creek. And that got me to thinking.

Now, the sounds of a creek or brook, the burbling, rushing, miniscule roar of water on rock, could not be mistaken for the buzz of a gasoline motor turning a generator, but when it is fifty feet distant, it is not very dissimilar to the sound of swift traffic on a nearby highway. If you listen carefully, you can tell them apart, but if it is just background sound, they are much the same. But to me, the sound of the creek is a pleasure, while the sound of traffic is a pain.

Why?

This is not unique; there are many such pairs. The yips and howls of coyotes in the distance, and the barks and whines of dogs at the other end of the campground. The squeals and screams of children at play, and the shouts and shrieks of a husband and wife arguing. The bugling of elks in rut, and the bawling of a herd of cows. The bleating of deer, and the baaing of sheep. The crackle of a campfire, and the static on a radio. The rumble of thunder, and the grumble of a diesel big-rig. And not only of sounds: The taste of dissolved minerals in springwater, the taste of chlorine in tapwater; the sight of variegated vegetation in the forest wall, and the view of "artistic" patterns on the side of a motor home; the feel of a wave of pollen drifting among the pines, and the touch of a cloud of dust kicked up by an ATV. In all of these cases, the first is desireable, and the second is a nuisance.

Why?

From the purely physical aspect, the viewpoint of Physics, there is little or no difference between the members of these pairs. The reason must lie elsewhere, and the only alternate to physical is spiritual; it lies in the mind, not in the eye of the beholder, but in the world-view, the ideals, the consideration. You can call it preference, or prejudice, or standards, or bigotry; there are many fitting words. Which one best applies is, again, the individual's consideration. I have known people who hold the straight streets and rectilinear buildings of a city or town to be beautiful, and far preferable to the random and unplanned vistas of deserts and hills. I knew one man who admired regular orange groves and despised wild forests. I know bikers who revel in the (literally) deafening roars of their rides, and are contemptuous of the soft purr of my pipes. Are these people wrong? No, of course not. Just different.

Many people do not like waking to a frigid forty-degree morning. To them, it means something is wrong. Probably the furnace has broken down. I do not enjoy being cold, but I like the cold mornings because I know how to dress for it and be warm, and it makes the morning campfire more enjoyable, in the same way a beer tastes better when you are thirsty. I like the sound of the creek, because I associate it with the creek itself and with the peaceful and comfortable environs. I associate coyotes with openness and freedom, and child-noises with happiness and wonder; they are sharing my world, and that makes my world better. There are bigots who insist that their view is the correct one. Not better, not an alternative, but *the* correct view. Everyone else is wrong. There are prejudiced people who hold their view because they were told to hold it; people they respected said it was correct or best, and they, without thinking or evaluating, accepted and believed it. There are people who hold their views by association; they dislike snow because they once came near to freezing to death, so snow means danger, or they are uncomfortable in the woods because as children they were frightened by a bear, and they know the woods are full of bears. Many of my views were formed like this. I told you why I like stream-sounds; traffic-sound is reminiscent of the dreadful decades I lived in a city.

Better is to evaluate: You dislike a thing. Why? Because it feels bad, because it is not pleasing, because it is different, because it reminds of something or someone, whatever. If you understand your preference, the undesireable becomes less bad, and may even become pleasant, and the desireable usually becomes better. But you do not have to bother with that; while understanding is always good, the more important thing is enjoyment. If you like it, if it brings you pleasure, it is good. It is just esthetics.

And besides, you need bad to enhance good. The happiest man is the one who knew the worst misery, and has risen from that. No one appreciates water more than the person who almost died of thirst.

Magic in Nebraska

I have spent several months in the mountains of Colorado and Wyoming, and I am now heading for the Black Hills in South Dakota. The route I have chosen crosses Nebraska for the most part. It is a gradual change; the hills slowly grow lower, the trees fewer, the grass yellower. It takes a few dozen miles to really flatten out, but then I am in the prairie; miles and miles of grass, the only fencing being the right-of-way for the road. Open. Flat. Not mountains. Wow!

Soon I get used to land where you can't lie down while still standing up, and realize this part of Nebraska is *not* flat. It's all hills, long, very long, smooth, gradual; you can barely justify using the word "climb". And it is not forest, it is all grass. Occasionally there is a copse, half a dozen or twenty trees, then after a half mile or three, perhaps another. Or not. Often it is only grass, tall grass, clear to the horizon in all directions. If there are bushes, they are hiding in the taller grass. Aside from the road, with its companion fence and line of power poles, there is nothing but grass. No house or barn or windmill. No cattle or deer or birds. No trees. No rocks. Only grass and sky.

Beautiful grass! Magnificent grass! Green and yellow and brown, tall, and rippling and waving as the wind rides it across the plain. These are the "amber waves of grain" in Momma Nature's farm.

Over a ridge, the world changes. To the East, a giant machine traverses the field, leaving in its path a neat lawn and man-high cylinders of what was once grass, now transformed into hay. To the West stands an ocean of rich green worthy of Ireland, corn, maize, the Indian grain, tall, proud, thick, an impenetrable glory of abundance, the true Emerald City. Of a certainty, there is Magic in this land.

The farmed land continues. There are pastures bounded by fences, planted fields, recently plowed, half-grown, ripe or harvested. And they are huge, huge! It seems the smallest is a half-mile long! A deer stands alone in the midst of stubble, more than a mile from the nearest tree. In the far distance, a dozen Winkies or Munchkins stand by a green truck. Or maybe they are human, and it is a harvester or a combine. No. This day is too magical. They must be Munchkins. I'll bet they are wearing blue.

On and on I follow the Gray Tar Road; at least it has a yellow line in the middle. The cultivated land falls behind, an island in the boundless ocean of grass. The ridges become more pronounced, and larger, great ocean swells, two or three miles from crest to crest. On some of the crests, whitecaps of bedrock break through.

The air grows hotter, the sun more intense. In the heat and the dryness the road ahead shines like a lake. It is the Mirage, which lured so many pioneers to their deaths, for to a thirsty man, it is a promise of water. It *looks* like water, you can *see* it, it's *right there,* only a mile away. But it is always a mile away, always there, never, ever, here. He saw water because he wanted to see water. If you really look at it, though, the mirage does not look like water. It is the sky, reflected in the mirror which the heat has made of the road. Look closely; you will see clouds and even trees from the horizon, if there are any, and if the angle is right. When the sky is lonesome and pure, as it is today, the Mirage is actually a piece of the sky, fallen by accident, perhaps, or possibly visiting its friend, the Earth. Or maybe . . .

Maya, the Indians say (the ones on the other side of the world), illusion. All the world is illusion, only here because we perceive it, because we say it is here. Do not scoff! There are a billion who believe it, and they may be right. As I drop into the valley, the crest of the horizon becomes a dam, holding back the ocean of sky. Where the road touches the horizon, the mirage forms. The road breeches the dam, and the sky flows down, a river flooding the land, pouring in, erasing the Earth. I charge up the rise, banner flying, and the invading blue army hesitates, stops, slowly retreats. As I approach the crest, the road reforms for me and is intact and solid as I cross the horizon. A new valley lies before me, with a new horizon. The plains are where they should be, the sky is where it belongs. As long as I have new horizons, I am content.

But this day is truly magical, and I am watching.

About the Author

The Lonesome Hillbilly is a wanderer from birth. Born in the Lone Star Republic (but not in Texas), he traveled a thousand miles by his first birthday, and ten thousand by his second. He lives on a motorcycle, and in a tent he made. He has been in every state of the Union, plus Asia and Europe. Politically he is a Rational Anarchist. Spiritually, he respects all religions, and no churches. He winters in the low deserts of Arizona, and tours all New Mexico during the Spring. The rest of the time, you will find him somewhere within five hundred miles of the Rocky Mountains. Probably.

Stay Free!

www.ingramcontent.com/pod-product-compliance
Lightning Source LLC
Chambersburg PA
CBHW061805250726
48657CB00001B/286